The Spirit-led Student

My Journey Out of Performance and into His Presence with Joy

By Veronica Karaman

Note: All scripture references are from the
New International Version, unless otherwise noted.
KJV = King James Version
AMP = Amplified Version

Table of Contents

Dedicated to my mother, Mildred Karaman, who never had the chance to pursue an education, but showed me the way to being a true champion. To all His students who desire to maximize their learning potential in partnership with the Great Professor.

May you know the joy of learning as you enter into study as worship.

Foreword

"Do not conform any longer to the pattern of this world,
but be transformed by the renewing of your mind." (Romans 12:2a)

The great calling of the Christian student is not only to educate his mind, but to renew his mind. While the world's academic system beckons and even enslaves a student to "make the grade" as the seeming do-all, end-all goal, God's standard for a student goes much higher. In fact, it goes so much higher that it is as radically different from our perceived values of what an education is all about, as a bicycle is from a space rocket. God's way for a student versus the world's way for a student is kingdoms apart.

As a fulfillment of the Great Commandment, we are called as God's students to love God with all our mind (Matthew 22:37). This standard is not based on a system of performance, but rather relationship. The goal of a Christian's education is to know God, to love God, and to love our neighbor as ourselves (John 17:3, Matthew 22:39). The earmark of the Christian student's experience is the eternal difference walking with God in academics makes as opposed to learning in independence from God with a grade as your main marker for learning.

When a student is bound by the limits of "academic law," she is trapped into a system that is motivated by fear and anxiety. When I ask high achieving college students to describe in one word what it is like to learn at their university, the number one answer I get is "anxiety." God never designed you to learn in anxiety! He designed you to learn in His presence, marked by the atmosphere of His Kingdom, which is righteousness, peace, and joy in the Holy Spirit (Romans 14:17).

The Good News is there is an escape plan for you from the fear, anxiety, stress, and lack of meaning you experience in school! If you are a son or daughter of God, God has already delivered you out of the world of darkness and into the light! I often tell students, the only way out of a system is with another system. The moment you accepted Christ as your Savior, He delivered you from all the world's systems and made you a citizen of His Kingdom. You have a new birthright to learn in peace, joy, and the eternal presence of God Himself, the Greatest Professor of All. Your goal is no longer excellence, but wholeheartedness. It is to enter into learning as a partnership with God. It's not just about a grade. It's about Him!

For over the last twenty-five years, I have had the privilege of ministering to students a biblical approach to study which is life-giving and freeing. I have seen thousands of students move from the crippling effects of performance to soaring with God through the mysteries of learning. Each time the transfer from the world's ways to God's ways takes place in learning, there is always a testimony of liberation and excellence of achievement, sometimes to the utter astonishment of the student. What would you learn about yourself, God, and others---what could you achieve---if you were set free from fear and anxiety, and had fresh creativity available to you along with the wisdom of the Creator of the Universe? What would happen to your passion for learning and meaning in life? How much more could you maximize your learning potential studying in partnership with the Source of All Knowledge Himself? Entering into a partnership with God in your learning is your supernatural advantage as a Christian student.

Little did I know as I pursued God in my academics way back in the mid 1980's that God was working on birthing a ministry to students through me based on the truths He was working on in my life.

My graduate thesis was entitled, "Spirit-led Study." I developed a course called "The Renewed Mind in Academics," training students how to be led by the Holy Spirit in their studies. I have taught that course to thousands of students over the years at all levels, from junior high to post-doctoral. I later changed the name to *God's Way to an A*.

I wrote this book because we have learned to apprehend God and His truths in many areas of our lives, including finances, relationships, work, and health. However, when it comes to study and the process of learning, most approaches to integration are intellectual, not devotional. When students come to realize they have left God out of their study process, the light bulb comes on. Their automatic response is, "Why, I never thought of including God in my studies! I include Him in all other areas of my life!" It's as if the enemy of their soul has blinded them to the wondrous relationship awaiting them in this area of their lives, too. And the truth is, he has.

This book is about my journey of coming to know the love of God in my studies while in graduate school at Regent University. It is about my coming to know the Holy Spirit as my Teacher, in the midst of crying out to God for wisdom, direction, and fulfillment in lieu of not having those natural guidance counselors to help me find God's path for my life.

It's a personal look into the inner workings of God and how He brings transformation in the life of a student-seeker who desperately needed a new identity based on His unconditional love and not a faulty, performance-based system which only brings death and destruction ultimately.

My heart is for you to see who God can be to you in your studies by seeing how God worked in my own life as a student. It's for you to see that your struggle in school is meant to be more than a chore, but an adventure with God who is interested in building a whole new foundation in your life—one that is eternal.

It is my prayer and deep desire that as you read this account of my walk with Jesus through my studies, you will see how much God loves you and wants to use you - right where you are - to raise a new standard in your life and to those around you. May you also come to see that God is not separate from education, but the Author behind it all. He invites you into His presence to tutor you through each step of your learning journey.

As you enter into God's classroom, it is my prayer that your aim would be to embrace the two greatest commandments, "Love the Lord your God with all your heart and with all your soul and with all your mind" and "Love your neighbor as yourself" (Matthew 22:37,39).

I pray for your spiritual eyes to be opened to who God can be to you in your studies. There is a great adventure filled with joy awaiting you as you renew your mind to the presence and power of God in your academics. This book is about running my academic race with God. So now I am passing the baton on to you. Now run with it!

March 2015
Veronica Karaman

CHAPTER ONE

BUILDING ON A FAULTY FOUNDATION

"Therefore let us leave the elementary teachings about Christ and go on to maturity, not laying again the foundation of repentance from acts that lead to death." (Hebrews 6:1)

Ever since I can remember, I have always pursued excellence and wanted to be the best, even as a little girl. Although I do not know where that drive came from, I have spent a lifetime trying to understand both the gift and the downfall of a relentless drive for achievement.

My first recollection of wanting to excel was on the golf course. When I was five years old my father placed a putter in my hand. He was a weekend player who loved the game as a recreational pursuit. Even at that young age, however, my love for the game went far beyond a mere pastime.

My summertime passion was to win the national Pee-Wee Putting contests that my father entered me in for nine years in a row. Every time we would go to the golf course, my father would play for four hours, while I stayed on the putting green and putted for four hours. My desire to compete and be the best went hand-in-hand with the development of my game.

1

When I was fourteen years old I took up the whole game of golf. Growing up in western Pennsylvania, I could not play year-round, so I crammed my summer days with swinging the club from sun up to sundown. My mother drove the forty-five minute trip to the golf course at seven o'clock in the morning to drop me off and then returned to pick me up at dark. My regular routine was to play at least thirty-six holes a day. Sometimes I even played fifty-four holes in one day.

My intense desire to excel and be the best paid off in becoming an excellent amateur player. I had the opportunity to play great golf courses and I became a local celebrity athlete. In high school I played on the boys' team and I was the first female graduate in my school to win an athletic scholarship to college.

My desire to be the best and to perform with excellence went beyond the golf course and into the classroom. Even at five years old in kindergarten I had to be first. First in line. First on the bus. First to raise my hand in class.

In third grade, I remember I had to be first when it came to grades. It was nothing for me to study for a geography test for three hours to be sure I knew everything. Whenever I missed even one point, I asked the teacher what I did wrong. In fifth grade, I practiced my multiplication tables for hours at home. It was important for me to do 100 multiplication questions in less than a minute. To be the first one to raise my hand when I finished the test was my aim and joy.

It was always a joy for me to excel, to win a golf tournament, or to graduate at the top of my class. Nothing is wrong with that. In fact, I believe God instills within people the desire to achieve. After all, nobody sets out to be a failure.

However, there was a problem with all my competitiveness and perfectionism. It had become addictive. My self-worth became tied up with my performance. Deep on the inside, I *had* to perform and

2

excel to feel good about myself. Fear of failure became my curse. Relationships became secondary. Soon I became a prisoner of my own making and I did not know how to escape. At age fifteen my problem was compounded with the death of my father.

The day after his funeral I went back to school to take a history exam. I just *had* to make a 100 per-cent on the exam. Nothing else would do. At the very moment I needed a hug, an embrace, and nurture from my mother to get me through the devastating loss of my father, I turned to achievement instead. My family never talked about emotions or worked through relational issues, so I never received any kind of help from Mom or others to work through my father's death. We never spoke about it, so the only way I knew how to survive was to perform.

What I needed most in my life was to know that I was loved unconditionally. I needed to know that I could fail and still be considered a wonderful person. I needed to know that a true foundation for life is in relationships, not achievement. Most of all, I needed to get in touch with the problem so that I could get free.

Every now and then while growing up I sensed that something was missing, and that I was building my life on the wrong kind of foundation. For example, when I realized I wasn't in a position to win my first golf tournament, I wanted to leave immediately. My reasoning was that if I wasn't going to finish first, there was no reason to hang around. It didn't dawn on me that remaining in the tournament would have provided me with valuable playing experience. It would have also given me the chance to meet new friends. But that benefit never entered my performance-oriented thinking. Sometimes I would feel terribly depressed, but I didn't know why. All I knew was that something was lacking.

At times on the golf course I would practice in a place where I was certain people could see me. "If somebody would only come over and watch me, just to be with me" was my heart's cry. My mother would often come with me to help pick up the golf balls, but even in that shared experience, something was missing. My deep need for acceptance was expressed in the classroom, too.

In eighth grade I decided to run for a student council office. Having more credentials than everyone else, I thought it would be a breeze to win the election. Furthermore, my girlfriend was a terrific artist, and she painted all kinds of cartoon characters on my election signs. Yes, I even had the best signs.

In the middle of the campaign, someone tore down all my signs. When I discovered who it was and turned the person in, nobody would talk to me. It was as if I had committed an injustice by telling the truth. A guy who couldn't even recite the pledge of allegiance ended up winning the election. Walking down the halls, I was devastated. No one supported me. I didn't understand how I could perform so well and be so empty on the inside.

On the outside there were great benefits to becoming a star student and athlete. I did not realize at the time that I was earning my way to a college scholarship to one of the best schools in the land, which I did not know even existed at the time.

My plan on graduating early from high school was to play golf and attend Duquesne University in my hometown of Pittsburgh in the fall, so I did not have to be far away from my mother. One weekend I received a phone call from a man who told me he was the athletic director from the University of Georgia who wanted to recruit me to the school. When I believed him, the voice on the other end of the phone started laughing. "Veronica, this is Bob, your friend!" I could have smacked him for tricking me into believing he was somebody he was not.

The very next weekend I received another phone call. "Veronica, this is the athletic director from Duke." I immediately thought it was Bob again, pulling another prank on me. "Cut it out, Bob!" I said. It really was the athletic director from Duke University! I did not even know about Duke. I thought it was short for Duquesne

University. Carl James went on to explain that he received some scholarship information about me from one of the ladies at my club, totally a surprise to me. "We would love for you to play golf at Duke. Can I send you an application?" I told him no. He called several more times.

Finally, I told him I would stop and look at the school on my way home from a vacation I was taking with my cousin in Florida. When I did visit the school, I realized what a fool I was to even refuse the first phone call. Duke gave me almost a full scholarship, and coupled with another scholarship, I ended up attending college on a full-ride.

It was as if a higher power was guiding me during this important life-transition from high school to college. While I chose one path that seemed to make sense to me, God in His sovereignty, had yet an even higher path for me. I did not choose my university. God chose my university for me, and made a way for me to go there when I did not even know Duke University existed. I was just beginning to experience the hand of my heavenly Father in my life.

While I excelled at golf at Duke, I was totally unprepared emotionally to attend college. I hid behind my athletics and academics because I had so many personal insecurities, although you would not know that from looking at me. My overachiever syndrome and lack of feeling unconditional acceptance were only magnified in college.

Furthermore, while at Duke I became very frustrated with my religious upbringing. My parents did an excellent job at raising me with a solid reverence for God, but I could not live up to all the demands I felt God was placing on me: "Go to church. Say your prayers. Be perfect." To me, everything was always black and white, so I became disillusioned when I saw religious leaders around me unable to uphold the most basic Christian standards. Not even my religious background offered any solace.

And then one day, everything changed.

CHAPTER TWO

A NEW BUILDER

"For no one can lay any foundation other than the one already laid, which is Jesus Christ." (1 Corinthians 3:11)

During the summer of 1980, I spent my time in Pinehurst, North Carolina. A charming and quaint town, Pinehurst is also known for being one of the golf capitals of the world. It was here that I met Jesus Christ as my Lord and Savior. He was no longer the disapproving, impossible-to-please Father in heaven. For the first time in my life He became a real and living person who loved me just as I was. It happened in the midst of my deep inner struggle.

One day I decided to visit a Christian bookstore. I had never been to a Christian bookstore before in my life! But that day I walked into the store and left with ten books on Christianity. I do not remember the titles of any of them, but what I do remember is what happened while reading them one night about two o'clock in the morning.

I was deep into a theologically-based book when I finally understood what Jesus Christ had done for me. "Jesus shed His blood on the cross, taking my sins upon Himself, so that I can be restored to fellowship with God and enter heaven! Salvation is a gift. There is nothing I can do to earn it. I just need to receive the finished work He has already accomplished for me." As I pondered that truth, I reached out to God from my heart and simply said, "Jesus, I need you." After inviting Him into my heart, I went to bed.

When I woke up the next morning all I could say was, "I've overcome!" All I could feel was joy! Something wonderful had happened to me. I was made new on the inside. All the years of searching had culminated in finding my answer. His name was Jesus.

Jesus not only made me new on the inside, He was getting ready to make everything new in my life, including my golf and my academics. What I was about to find out was that God was going to rebuild my life with a foundation that would last forever.

I began to feel inklings of His work while still a student at Duke. For three years I studied business and management science. I found all my classes were dull and boring. When I became a Christian just before my final year in college, I decided to take my first religion class. Something inside of me exploded! I actually felt a natural passion to study something, not based on a need to excel, but simply on a desire to know more about God. This was a brand new experience for me. I did not know if I should postpone my graduation to get a second major in religion. After meeting with Dr. Barney Jones, a wonderful professor who gave me great counsel, I decided to go ahead and graduate on time.

After I graduated in 1981, I decided to try the professional golf tour. For approximately one year I gave it my best shot, but all I experienced was more struggle. Feeling like I was always taking two steps forward and three steps backwards, I was tired of the tour grind. Furthermore, the burst of growth I felt when I first accepted Christ slowly eroded on the tour, simply because I had no place to get planted and lay a solid foundation as a Christian. Desiring to truly make Jesus the Lord of my life -- and not golf -- I decided to quit golf for good in the winter of 1982.

Little did I know both the challenge and adventure awaiting me.

CHAPTER THREE

BULLDOZING

"Unless the Lord builds the house, its builders labor in vain." (Psalm 127:1)

When God does a work, He starts from scratch. There is no "Hamburger Helper" in His kitchen. Nor is He in the household improvement business. If He comes to your life and finds work that needs to be done, He will tear down what is already there and build something entirely new, His way.

That means that when He comes into our lives His first order of business is to tear down old foundations and start fresh on level ground. If the ground is not level, He will bulldoze down every obstacle standing in the way of His new construction. He does this because He is interested in building things that will last for all eternity.

Perhaps you have felt the pain and the discomfort of God's "construction" in your life. For the nine months following my decision to quit golf, all I felt was God's holy bulldozer beginning to tear down my foundations of perfectionism and performance-orientation. Ouch! It hurt!

My hurt was the slicing away of my sense of identity. All I knew myself to be was a golfer. Not yet knowing who I was in Christ, I was confused and lacked direction.

Fortunately, I was in a good place for God to begin building right away. During this time I was living with my brother in Fayetteville, North Carolina. While attending his church, I became rooted in the Word of God, received great support from the pastor and the people, and became involved in leadership in the young adult group. But I wanted something more. I wanted some *action*, something that would give my life meaning, direction, and excitement.

So I began crying out to God. My desire to know what the next step was in my life drove me to spend more time praying and studying the Bible to try to find answers. One night I prayed, "Lord, I don't know what it means to hear from You. I do not know what Your voice even sounds like. But I am going to stay right here and start reading this Bible, and I will not stop until I hear from You."

For hours I read the Bible. After going through the book of Psalms, I read through Proverbs, Ecclesiastes, the Song of Solomon, and finally Isaiah. When I came to Isaiah 30:19, I burst into tears. God spoke the following verses directly to my heart:

> "O people of Zion, who live in Jerusalem, you will weep no more. How gracious he will be when you cry for help! As soon as he hears, he will answer you. Although the Lord gives you the bread of adversity and the water of affliction, your teachers will be hidden no more; with your own eyes you will see them. Whether you turn to the right or to the left, your ears will hear a voice behind you saying, 'This is the way; walk in it.'" (Isaiah 30:19- 21)

The scripture went on to say that I would throw away my idols, and God would bring restoration to my life. This scripture would become my life scripture. What God was saying to me was that He was going to lay down a whole new foundation in my life. That foundation would not be based on my performance or merit, but on the unconditional love and acceptance He provided for me through his Son Jesus Christ.

I would come to know that my heavenly Father would lead me and be with me each step of the way as I learned how to appropriate His love and acceptance in each area of my life, including my sport and academics. Only as I applied the truth to my life would I become free from my past bondages, allowing me at last to become all that God had destined me to become.

My focus began to change from one of merely performance to one of relationship. Instead of thinking only about how I could excel, I began to wonder, "How does God make a difference in my studies? Does God care enough to be with me in my golf?"

God not only heard my prayer for some "action," but He was about to answer one of my questions with an unexpected whirlwind of events.

CHAPTER FOUR

LAYING A NEW CORNERSTONE

"See, I lay a stone in Zion, a tested stone, a precious cornerstone for a sure foundation; the one who trusts will never be dismayed." (Isaiah 28:16)

One July morning in 1983, I tuned in to watch *The 700 Club* on television for the first time. During the show there was a thirty-second commercial highlighting CBN University (now Regent University). When I saw the campus, something inside of me ignited. I had never felt a spark in my spirit like that before. All I knew was that something deep inside of me lit up. I did not understand what the spark meant, but it definitely caught my attention. Not knowing how to interpret what I felt in my spirit, I soon forgot about that special moment.

Later that summer, I visited a friend of mine in Florida over Labor Day weekend. It was the last night of my visit. My friend and I were walking along the beach, brainstorming the potential opportunities I had for my life. The more we talked, the more I began to remember the excitement I felt a few months prior about the commercial for CBN University. As that excitement flooded back to me, I blurted out, "Do you know what I would like to do? I would like to visit CBN University." "Do it," he encouraged me.

Although the idea seemed a bit crazy since it was not in my agenda to return to graduate school, I did have the time to check things out. The next day I woke up feeling a great sense of adventure about the whole idea, so I jumped into my car and drove from Palm Beach, Florida, to Virginia Beach, Virginia! My deep desire to find God's plan for my life motivated me to take serious action!

Two days later, I arrived on campus. As I stepped out of my car, I felt like Columbus discovering America. I immediately knew I had found what I had been looking for all those months, even years. Walking around campus, my attention was drawn to the front steps of the network building where students and staff were gathered for a special time of worship and prayer. The presence of the Holy Spirit was so strong that I began to weep. As Pat Robertson was praying, God gave him a word of knowledge about the healing of someone's feet. Those feet happened to be mine!

At the time I was suffering from a lot of pain in my feet. The podiatrist said that my feet were imbalanced, my bones were falling apart, and I had the beginning of heel spurs. I had to wear plastic cups in my shoes to protect my heels from further injury. Nothing alleviated the pain. At that moment, however, God instantly healed my feet. The pain left and I have not had a problem since!

What a miraculous welcome! God had led me to the destination of his desire and was about to lay down a whole new foundation for my feet to walk on. More confirmation for my spontaneous "field trip" was on its way.

The next day I met with a professor about applying to the School of Communication. After my interview, we ended up sitting next to each other in the chapel service. Not only did this professor feel strongly about my coming to the university, but God did, too.

The president of the university, Dr. Gottier, was giving the chapel address. He spoke on the renewed mind. His message was captivating. I had never heard that a Christian could glorify God with her mind. "I can be a Christian, smart, and blond?" I thought. "This is great!" As the president spoke about how we could think the very thoughts of God, the professor suddenly began to write down some notes at a feverish pace. "Hmm," I thought, "I wonder what he's doing." After the talk, the professor leaned over to me and said, "This message is for you. I believe it is from the Lord." The paper read, "Lo, I have brought you here. I want you here. Trust in me. I'll make the way."

First God spoke to me through the healing of my feet. Now He spoke to me through another person. This kind of succession of confirmations had never happened to me before. I felt like I was out in the ocean riding a wave. Something was happening beyond my control and I was just trying to go with the flow. That flow continued as I went to the admissions office.

While I was waiting for someone to get me an application form to the university, three young men walked into the office. Not knowing any of them, we struck up a brief conversation. "Are you thinking about coming here?" they asked. "Yes, I think so," I replied. As we talked, I felt a strange tug in my heart to pay attention to what they had to say. Their bottom line response was, "Well, we all feel very strongly in our spirits that you should be here." Then they turned around and walked out the door. It was as if they were three angels sent from above to confirm to me, "This is the way, walk in it." Actually, I thought, "What else do I need, a bomb to drop on me? God obviously wants me here."

Friday night I walked around campus feeling totally amazed at all that happened in two days. I kept asking, "God, how could you love me so much?" I was overwhelmed and humbled that God answered my prayer for action and direction in such a miraculous and convincing way. With only a month and a half to go until the winter quarter started, I returned to Fayetteville where I continued to experience God's leading.

The first person I spoke with to find a place to live invited me to be her roommate. Then I found a job that would require ten days of training. My supervisor hired me regardless, knowing I would only be there for six weeks. A man from church offered to move all my things to Virginia in his van. It seemed like God was rolling out the red carpet for me to go back to school. If God was moving in such a pronounced way to get me to school, I wondered what He was going to do once I got there!

It was obvious to me that God had not only begun to bulldoze down my past foundations, but was clearing the ground to build something entirely new. One of the most evident proofs of His clearing every path for me to return to school, and giving me a new way of looking at my life, occurred in my final interaction with my golf sponsor.

As any college student knows, going to school costs a lot of money. I wanted to go to school with a clean slate financially, but I owed my golf sponsor several thousand dollars. It wasn't a hard and fast payback plan that we had agreed to, but I wanted to be totally free from the burden of my debt.

To go to school with the thought of owing anybody anything was a weight I did not want to carry. It was important to me to focus on my studies and what I was embarking upon. I did not want to carry anything into that place from my past. The only thing I knew to do was to ask my golf sponsor to forgive me of my debt. I was scared to death to face him on this issue, but somehow I mustered up enough courage to make the two hour drive to High Point.

My sponsor was the head of a world-famous furniture company. He loved golf and he was also a Duke University graduate. We met through the encouragement of the athletic director after I graduated. Although he was a warm and direct man, I did not know him very well. All I knew was that he gave me the opportunity to play professional golf, and now I was asking him to give me the opportunity to go to school debt-free.

As I walked into his presidential office, I swallowed hard. I said, "Sir, I've come here to ask you for your help." Explaining to him my desire to go back to school as financially free as possible, I quickly expressed the point of my visit: "Would you forgive me of my debt?" I knew that in his financial position the dollar amount would probably not be a big issue for him. It was the asking that bent me all out of shape. I wasn't used to admitting I needed help, especially when it involved telling someone I hadn't been able to accomplish what I had set out to do.

Without blinking an eye, he said yes. Another boulder was cleared out of the way for me to go back to school! Humbled and grateful, I thanked him and headed for the door to leave. Relieved, but feeling awkward, I didn't have anything more to say.

He did. "Veronica..." I turned around. "Yes, sir?" "Remember that I love you, Veronica." With tears in my eyes and inexpressible gratitude in my heart, I left his office.

My sponsor not only forgave me, he also told me he loved me. That spoke volumes to me. I was so used to a success/failure mentality about everything in my life that there was no room for grace. My sponsor's words meant that it was okay for me to try something and not succeed at it the way I had hoped to. I was still a valuable person. It wasn't the debt I owed that mattered most. He was in a financial position to cover the loss with little consequence on his part. What mattered most to him was that I knew I was loved and not a failure.

What I remember from that experience is not my golf performance, but the love and forgiveness expressed to me by my sponsor. To me, that was one of the most vivid demonstrations of the love and forgiveness of Jesus Christ Himself. It was as if God orchestrated this encounter with my sponsor right before I left for school as an awakening to the kind of foundation He was preparing to build in my life. That foundation would have as its chief corner-stone Jesus Christ, His love, and forgiveness.

One more sovereign event was still awaiting me before I left for school. It was this next encounter with God that revealed to me my part of the rebuilding process.

CHAPTER FIVE

MY FIRST BUILDING BLOCK

*"Now faith is being sure of what we hope for and certain
of what we do not see."* (Hebrews 11:1)

Two nights before I left for Virginia I attended an evangelistic service. The place was packed with people. I was sitting up front. There was only one empty seat in the whole place, and it was right next to mine.

During the offering time, the traveling evangelist gave specific instructions on how we were to give: "I am going to pray and ask God to put a number in your mind. Whatever that number is, that is what I want you to give."

The number "one hundred" came to my mind. Shocked, I quickly responded, "One hundred! God, I have never given a hundred dollars in my life. You know I'm saving up for school. Could this really be Your voice?" In my heart I knew if I heard $25 or less, that was God! Anything more, I'd really have to question it. Finally, I gave in and said, "Okay, God, if this is really You, please confirm it."

It was becoming obvious to me that God was trying to show me a new way of operating, based on my trust in Him, and not merely on my own resources. The challenge was scary to me because it was such a new thing for me to trust God beyond my comfort zone.

19

I don't know where she came from, but a little girl walked down the aisle. She was no more than seven years old. Crossing over the people to my right, she sat down in the empty seat next to mine. Placing her hand in mine, this young girl whispered into my ear "If you need a hundred, give a hundred."

I almost jumped out of my seat! Like an angel she whispered into my ear the confirmation I needed. Amazed, I grabbed my checkbook as tears streamed down my face. Then I decided this experience was too far out to give the check at offering time. I was going to give it to the evangelist in person after the service.

After telling the visiting minister what happened, he looked at me and said, "I will accept this money on one condition." I thought to myself, "An evangelist accepting money on condition. This is a new one." He went on to say, "I will accept this money if you will believe God to meet all of your needs on time." As I agreed with him that I could believe God to do that, I handed him my check.

This incident was my first major encounter with God in His teaching me how to walk by faith. It was also a very precious building block in my new way of living. I cannot underscore enough the significance of this event. God, my heavenly Father, was teaching me, His daughter, an eternal principle of seed faith. I was sowing now to reap something multiplied back to me later on. Moreover, God was showing me in this whirlwind of events that the way I would approach my life from now on would be from a standpoint of trusting in my relationship with God, not in my own performance. The days ahead would require such a trust.

CHAPTER SIX

SEEKING AND FINDING

"Come, all you who are thirsty, come to the waters; and you who have no money, come, buy and eat! Come, buy wine and milk without money and without cost. Why spend money on what is not bread, and your labor on what does not satisfy? Listen, listen to me, and eat what is good, and your soul will delight in the richest of fare. Give ear and come to me; hear me that your soul may live." (Isaiah 55:1-3a)

Labor Day weekend 1983 was a turning point in my life that set me on the path back to graduate school. In retrospect, I now understand that the series of events that led to my discovery of the new foundation and plan that God had for my life didn't happen by chance. Nor did they happen by God simply reaching down His omnipotent hand, grabbing me by the collar, and forcing me to go where He wanted me to go.

I found myself getting in tune with the will of God because I chose to put my hand in His and walk with Him. Cooperating with God is the key. Because God is sometimes not easy to know or understand, discovering His will and ways require wholehearted searching. That search can be the result of frustration, desperation, or a simple, intense desire to please the Lord.

In observing the study habits of hundreds of students, I have found that all too many let their frustration and struggle with school cause them to give up. They come to the end of themselves and quit. The quitting point in the flesh, however, is precisely the starting point with God. I found this to be true in my own life. It seemed that I had to have my back against the wall before I would look up and trust God. Every time I looked up in those situations, I found an overhead door open to me, with His voice saying, "Come up a little higher, Veronica. You're spending your labor on what does not satisfy. Walk with Me and I'll show you My way."

What do you do when you are frustrated in your work? Do you turn to God? Or, do you turn to some form of escape or relief? Do you simply look to the limitations of your own resources, or do you allow your limitations to motivate you to look to God?

As I write this chapter, I am sitting at the dining room table. Directly in view as I gaze out the window is the 14th tee at Suntree Country Club. Every five minutes or so a group of golfers arrives to tee off. I have observed every kind of swing imaginable: choppy, overextended, stiff, loopy, and a few graceful ones. One guy just drilled the ball about thirty yards.

The reaction to every poorly hit shot is some expression of frustration: pounding the club on the turf, a disgruntled look at the golfer's playing partner, an embarrassed sigh, a quick walk back to the cart. It is my professional guess that few of the golfers ever allow their frustration to motivate them to go get some instruction. Why? Because it will require change. It will require work and practice, practice, practice. But it will also bring eventual reward, greater understanding of the correct way to swing, lower scores, elimination of much frustration, and greater overall pleasure in their ball-striking ability. Sometimes it takes a long time for a golfer to finally seek out instruction.

Likewise, sometimes it takes us a long time to turn our full attention to God. We will chop, slice, and overexert our way through school, or whatever God has called us to, never once thinking to allow our frustration to lead us to God for instruction. For me as a student, it took a whole year to look to God.

During that year I experienced a lot of frustration in my assignments, although I did well and enjoyed learning. I can remember how I was given an assignment in one class to write a ten page paper. My attitude toward writing the paper was, "If I have to lock myself in my room for ten hours to write this paper, I will." And that's exactly what I did. I felt like I was in prison and didn't know how to escape.

I wondered if there was a better, more fulfilling way to study. After all, I was promised an abundant life as a Christian, but my study experience was anything but "abundant and fulfilling." I was yearning to know if and how God had a way for me to study that was different than the world's way.

Three times in the opening verses of Isaiah 55, God gives the answer to the unsatisfied, restless heart. He says to "come." As I heard one Bible scholar describe it, the way out is in. In other words, the way out of your unfulfilling, frustrating situation is to come in closer to God and listen to His voice. In doing so, He will turn your unprofitable labor into a richness of soul (vs.2).

I decided to "come to God' through fasting on Labor Day weekend 1984. During my fast, God answered my prayers in a profoundly personal and unexpected way. My seeking had led finally to my finding!

CHAPTER SEVEN

A CALL TO REPENTANCE

"Let the wicked forsake his way and the evil man his thoughts. Let him
turn to the Lord, and he will have mercy on him...for he will freely
pardon. For my thoughts are not your thoughts, neither are your ways
my ways,' declares the Lord." (Isaiah 55:7, 8)

God knows how to speak to each one of us in such a way that we know His voice when He is talking. After three days of fasting, God once again spoke to me out of his word. I opened up five different Bibles to the same scripture. The scripture that hit my heart was Proverbs 11:1: "A false balance is abomination to the Lord" (KJV).

God showed me that basically I was using the wrong kind of standards or measurement in my studies. In other words, my standards were different than His. My standard was how many A's I could make. His standard was the extent to which I would allow the Holy Spirit to bear fruit in my life. I was placing too much stock in performance and temporal goals. What He wanted was for me to place primary emphasis on things of eternal importance.

By relying on grades as my standard of excellence and worth, I was actually engaging in idolatry. I was looking to performing well as an act of "works righteousness." I began to understand that up until this point, my motivation for doing school work was to earn a pat on the back from God when I did well. I was also expecting people to look at me and say, "Isn't she special? She does so well in school." Further conviction hit my heart when I realized that most of my reason for doing well was still based on a spirit of competitiveness. If I did better than everyone else, God would be pleased. In actuality, God considered all of this garbage. I didn't need to appease Him with anything. He did not want me to work *for* Him. What He wanted was for me to allow Him to work *through* me! My own self-righteousness was hindering the fullness of what God desired for me.

There was more understanding to come as a result of my fasting and God's revealing Himself to me. Studying was not to be an act of striving. Being a student was a calling. Just as some are called to be teachers, preachers, administrators, etc., God's perfect will for students while they are in school is to be His students. That's it. "Whatever you do, work at it with all your heart, as working for the Lord, not for men" (Colossians 3:23). My efforts were to be dedicated to the Lord, not to gain His approval of me. They were to be an act of profound thanksgiving for what Jesus had done for me. By His death on the cross, Jesus made it possible for me to be in right relationship with God. The ultimate goal of my education then, was not grades, but to walk in partnership with God in my studies. Again, God was impressing upon me that my focus was not the task, but Him. I was catching the revelation that academics was actually a form of worship as I consecrated my mind to learn my subjects *with* Him.

I cannot underscore enough the significance of this point. The ultimate aim of my education was not knowledge for knowledge's sake. The ultimate aim of my education was to know God. A great education and excellent grades would follow.

My mindset was beginning to change. I began to:

1. Think of Jesus as my study buddy or to think of the Holy Spirit as my Teacher.

2. Pray and praise God before doing assignments.

3. Be open to the unexpected.

4. Pray for the anointing. Both anointing -- the supernatural blessing of the presence of the Holy Spirit to accomplish some God-given task -- and skill are necessary for excellence in God.

Once God showed me how far I had moved away from His design for me as a student, I had no choice but to repent. I realized that I was walking independently of God in this area of my life. Even when independence is subtle or unintentional, it still qualifies as sin. Sin keeps us from walking in harmony with God's perfect ways for us. When God impressed on me that the reason I was so frustrated in my studies was because I had not leaned on the Holy Spirit as my Teacher, I understood my experience of frustration.

As new creatures in Christ, our spirit man is made alive to God. Going about my studies in worldly ways could only lead to struggle and striving because unconsciously I was trying to do something as a new creature using old creature ways. It's like trying to get a computer printout from stone tablets and a chisel. It just doesn't jive. Making Jesus Christ Lord in my academic life was the answer.

My prayer was, "Lord, please forgive me for walking in independence of You in my studies. I want to be led by the Holy Spirit in my studies, but nobody has ever taught me how. I don't know what it means to bear fruit as a student, but show me. Please teach me. I want to exalt You, and not my academic performance. Amen."

My act of repentance put me in a position to receive from God in a whole new and exciting way.

CHAPTER EIGHT

CONFIDENCE IN CHRIST

"As the heavens are higher than the earth, so are my ways higher than your ways and my thoughts than your thoughts." (Isaiah 55:9)

At the time I repented for walking in my own self-effort in my studies, I had signed up to take an acting class with Dr. Elaine Shouse. Dr. Shouse was known as a tremendous discipler. By the time you finished her classes, you either grew in the Spirit by at least a foot, or you wanted to throw a brick at her. She was someone who spoke the truth in love. Her innermost desire was to see us mature in Christ as we learned our academic disciplines. Now she was to be my teacher in a subject I had never studied before.

As I walked into my first acting class, I quickly peered around the room to check out the other students. It was obvious that I was surrounded by many experienced actors and actresses. Never having acted in my life, I was scared. Although I had never lacked self-confidence in my studies before, this time was different. My immediate reaction was to drop the course.

I decided to talk it over with Dr. Shouse. I told her, "I'm really concerned about how well I'll do in this class since I don't feel I have many natural abilities in this area. I'll have to work extra hard to do well. In fact, I'm considering dropping the course. What do you think?" In typical Christian professorial style, she encouraged me to go home and pray about it.

29

Driving home, I prayed. "God, I have no self-confidence in this class." God's response startled me. The answer He impressed upon me was, "Veronica, you are exactly where I want you to be, with no self-confidence. I want you to learn how to have confidence in Christ. I want to teach you how to cross over the bridge to the land of the Holy Spirit. Quit debasing yourself. Will you allow Me to be your source of confidence?"

That was not the answer I anticipated. The only way I could relate to what God was telling me was in remembering an incident that happened to me as a child.

In the neighborhood where I grew up there was a pack of about eight kids. Living on a short dead-end street we did everything together. We played together, slept over at one another's homes, and of course, fought with each other. One night, Francis, one of the kids, started a fight with a new neighbor. When the new neighbor's father came down to try and break up the fight, it only became more intense. I wanted to do something, but I was afraid I'd get hurt, too. Running into our house, I shouted for my dad. As I walked out of the house with my dad, my trembling heart became more than confident. Why? I was with my dad who could punch out anyone! I confidently strutted over to the scene of the potential fight. Within minutes my dad had taken charge and diffused any chances of a skirmish. Where I had been filled with fear standing by myself, I was filled with confidence with my hand in my dad's.

Perhaps that was what God was trying to get across to me. As I placed my hand in my heavenly Father's, my inadequacy about my acting class would be transformed into a hearty confidence in His ability. My focus would be on my relationship with Him and not on my own inadequacies.

The first action I took was to make a commitment to the course. "God, I don't know how to walk with You in my studies. Nobody has ever taught me, but I will stay in the class." The next thing I did was to pray over every detail of an assignment. "HELP! Jesus, please show me how to do this accent. What costume should I wear? How do I interact with the other characters?" I began including God in all my thoughts, talking to Him and asking Him for His help, and that began to transform my lack of confidence into something beautiful for God.

God made sure I knew that He was there with me every step of the way. My walk with Him in this class was certainly a test of faith.

One test of my faith came when I received a B+ on a drama performance when I thought I deserved an A. My journal entry for that day summed up my thoughts: "Lord, I am learning to make you my source of confidence. Although I received a lower grade than I wanted on this performance, I place my trust in You. Finding my security and identity in good grades is a real bondage. Thank you that You are most pleased when I am endeavoring to be led by your good Spirit in my academics."

God used my studies to show me more about myself, and more about Him. He did this not only through my performances, but through preparing for my tests.

Midterm time rolled around quickly. I had always studied hard. I relied on reviewing my notes just before each exam as my source of confidence. My circumstances during the day of the midterm, however, prevented me from practicing this normal routine for my "proper preparation." Little did I know that the Holy Spirit was about to teach me an even "higher way" of preparing for my exams.

It was pouring down rain that day. I was in the administration building. When I discovered that I had left my books and notes in the library, I began to panic! Without an umbrella, it was impossible for me to run back to the library to retrieve my notes. With only thirty minutes until exam time, I remembered that my new "Study Buddy" was present. I began to pray.

At that moment, I realized I had always depended on reviewing my notes for confidence in taking an exam. Although it was very important for me to study to prepare for an exam, I realized that the Holy Spirit was asking me to put more trust in Him as my confidence. It was as if the Holy Spirit were saying to me, "Veronica, didn't you ask Me to teach you how to depend on Me in your studies?" My reaction was, "Yes, but this is real!! I have a test in thirty minutes!"

I realized God had backed me into a corner and taken away my crutches. I had the choice of falling flat on my face or leaning on Him for support. Reluctantly, I gave in and said, "Okay, Holy Spirit, I am not going to rely upon the review of my notes as my source of confidence. I am deciding to rely upon You...whatever that means."

The Holy Spirit showed me that it is not what you rely on, but whom you rely on. He wanted me to rely on Him, whether it was in hearing His voice telling me how to study, or whether it was in walking into a situation resting totally on His grace and favor.

Having made my decision to rely upon the Holy Spirit, I took the test. It was one of those tests in which I could have done very well or very poorly. Leaving the class, all I felt was a lot of tension, knowing that I was still holding onto my grades for my self-esteem.

Walking across campus, I hung my head down low. "God, why do I feel so bad about myself? I feel like the way I did when I had a poor golf score. I want to go bury my head in the sand, like an ostrich. Please set me free." I felt the Lord's quick response: "Veronica, if you were a mother and had a child who just came home from school and told you she was disheartened about her performance on a test, what would you do? You knew that she prepared for it as well as she could." My response was, "God, I would just put her in my lap, hold her, and say, 'Honey, that's okay. I love you just the same.'" "That's exactly what my response is to you as your heavenly Father, Veronica. I love you and nothing will ever change that. Now hold your head up high."

In the midst of my discouragement, God was beginning to break through my works-orientation with His unconditional love.

A few days later Dr. Shouse called me aside for a personal discussion. I wondered what I had done wrong. Her comment was, "Veronica, I just wanted you to know that you passed the test with flying colors. You made the highest grade in the class." Even though I struggled with turning my studies over to God, He revealed His love and faithfulness to me in an overwhelming and delightfully surprising way.

He was to prove Himself to me one more time in my acting class. In my final class performance, I worked in partnership with another actress. We both felt inadequate in portraying our characters. We prayed over every detail, asking God to show us what to do. After much prayer, I still had some fear. It's the kind of fear that makes you think that you are going to forget your lines and make a fool out of yourself. I was reminded of Zechariah 4:6, "'Not by might, nor by power, but by my Spirit,' says the Lord."

Surprisingly, the performance was anointed and successful. It was the first time in years that I felt successful at something new. It was a small thing, but significant. Dr. Shouse gave me a tremendous compliment. She said that I was the most teachable student she ever had. It gave me a lift, but humbled me, too. I knew a lot of what she saw was just my simple, but wholehearted desire to learn how to follow God's ways in my schoolwork. My acting partner was equally blessed.

The biggest surprise came when the most experienced actress in the class made her way over to me. This was the actress against whom I compared myself the first day of the class. Her comment just about floored me: "Veronica, I never cry, but when you were up there performing, I had tears streaming down my face." The best actress in the class was commending me when I had felt like anything but an actress when I first entered the class.

I knew the anointing made up for a lack of experience, although I worked very hard on my performance. God's "higher ways" included the anointing.

Throughout the Bible, God gave His anointing to individuals. The very first person recorded in the Bible to be filled with the Spirit of God was a craftsman. "Then the Lord said to Moses, 'See I have chosen Bezalel...and I have filled him with the Spirit of God, with skill, ability and knowledge in all kinds of crafts - to make artistic designs for work in gold, silver and bronze, to cut and set stones, to work in wood, and to engage in all kinds of craftsmanship'" (Exodus 31:1-5).

In the above scripture we can see that the excellence of God involves both skill and anointing. Skill does not replace anointing. Anointing does not replace skill. One is based on our abilities. The other is based on God's special touch.

That extra touch of God, indefinable in human terms, but undeniably real, came as I spent time including God in my practice sessions. Increased confidence came as I saw God begin to work in a very real way in my studies.

My final grade for the course was an A. God was faithful and true to me when I didn't think that I had what it took to even stay in the class. What I remember most about the class is 'not the A, but what the A represented: the fact that God would show Himself faithful to me in my academics. In other words, I came to know God in a whole new way in the midst of my studies.

Isaiah 55:9 says that God's thoughts are vastly different than ours. They are as high above our thoughts as the heavens are higher than the earth. God's higher thoughts toward me were that I would know His love and faithfulness, and not just how to get good grades. Both of these would go hand in hand as I put my trust in Him.

My experience was so rewarding that I began to pray that other students would begin to know God in the same kind of way as I was coming to know Him. I wondered what kind of academic adventure was awaiting them if they would only dare to venture out with God. I would soon have my chance to find out.

CHAPTER NINE

THE ONLY THING GREATER THAN EXPERIENCE

"As the rain and snow come down from heaven and do not return to it without watering the earth and making it bud and flourish, so that it yields seed for the sower and bread for the eater, so is my word that goes out of my mouth: It will not return to me empty, but will accomplish what I desire and achieve the purpose for which I sent it." (Isaiah 55:10, 11)

The world will tell you that the way to accomplishment is to set a goal in your mind and then set out in your own strength to achieve that goal. Positive thinking is extremely important. Exertion of self-effort is key. The more experience you get, the greater your chances of success.

Although experience and effort are necessary ingredients to success, they are not the most important, according to biblical standards. The most essential ingredient for success in God is to get in touch with God's thoughts and purposes for a particular matter. When we align ourselves to God's thoughts, we will be assured of His success. Whatever He wills, He brings to pass. Getting into God's flow, instead of presumptuously expecting Him to get into ours, should be our primary concern. God never fails. Whatever He purposes, He fulfills.

Furthermore, God is the most experienced Person in the world.

He's been here before the beginning. As children of God, we have the privilege of sitting in His lap and learning from Him. As one of my professors put it, the only thing greater than experience is revelation. The Bible is full of God's revelation to His people on how to be successful and how to avoid what will cause unnecessary harm or effort on our part.

Consider the story of the Old Testament prophet Daniel. In my opinion, Daniel is the model student of the Bible. Six hundred years before the time of Christ, we find a young man who exemplifies a godly student.

When Jerusalem was besieged by King Nebuchadnezzar, Daniel was taken exile to Babylon along with some other young Hebrew men of nobility. For three years he studied the words and ways of an idolatrous people. During his time at the University of Babylon, Daniel refused to compromise in his relationship with God. Not partaking of the king's rich food and wine was Daniel's way of remaining obedient to his God and His commands. As a result of Daniel's resolve to be uncompromising, God responded by giving Daniel supernatural enablement to accomplish His divine purpose in Daniel's life.

In my opinion, Daniel 1:17 is the most powerful scripture a Christian student can embrace: "To these four young men God GAVE knowledge and understanding of all kinds of literature and learning."

Could you use a little supernatural enablement from God to understand your field of study? Remember Daniel was not studying the Bible. He was studying secular subjects and languages. God *gave* him wisdom and understanding to excel in his academics. Daniel did not earn this. He did not work extra hard to attain the favor of God, although I'm sure he was dedicated to his task. I believe Daniel's uncompromising faithfulness to God, coupled with a heart open to receiving from God, gave him the anointed edge.

We read in chapter two that when Daniel received the interpretation of the king's dream, he praised God for the answer. In his praise we find the concept of God as Revealer: "He gives wisdom to the wise and knowledge to the discerning. He reveals deep and hidden things; he knows what lies in darkness, and light dwells with him. You have made known to me what we asked of you" (Daniel 2:21b-22,23b).

We may safely surmise that Daniel exalted God as a student and later as a statesman. His motivation was not self-centered. All his efforts and success were a result of the greatness of his God.

One day as I was walking to chapel I was hit with a startling revelation of the motivation of my own heart. Although God had already revealed to me that my studying was done for the wrong reasons, something else occurred to me. In most other areas of my life, I was a Christian still living a self-centered lifestyle. Being a Christian rarely extended much beyond my own interests. There was a gap between what I saw in the character of Daniel and my own tainted soul. "Give me your heart, God," I prayed, "that I may be motivated by You and walk fully in Your ways. Fill me with Your wisdom."

God heard my prayer. It wasn't long before Spiritual Emphasis Week 1984 rolled around. One year prior on this weekend, God healed my feet and gave me a new foundation to walk on. This particular year He would use me to point others to a new path to walk on. The night before the weekly chapel service I prayed, "God, please give me a chance to share in chapel at least a few of the things You are showing me in my studies. The university would be greatly blessed by another affirmation of how You work."

My chance came. After worship, someone shared the scripture from Isaiah 30:19-21. My life scripture! I lowered my head and began to cry. The president of the university asked if anyone had anything to share. Too scared to walk to the podium on my own, I asked God to do something. The next thing I knew the president looked at me and said, "Veronica, do you have something to share?"

For a few minutes I shared: "God has been showing me that the only thing greater than experience is revelation. If we will seek Him as His students, He will reveal to us how to study, when to study, and free us from the chains of performance-orientation. He wants to reveal truth to us. Truth is not something that is earned. It is revealed. If we will learn how to make God our source of wisdom, and receive from Him, our university would be charged with intellectual and spiritual electricity like none other."

Sometime later a business student stopped me in the hall. He said that since he took hold of what I shared in chapel that his grades kept getting better and better. He was making A's in classes where he had not made A's before. Later he wrote me a short testimony:

"My wife and I came to the university and both enrolled in respective graduate programs. Along with our furnishings came our three children: ages 9, 7, and 4. We both worked full-time jobs and attended classes approximately three evenings per week between the two of us. We never utilized the services of a babysitter, feeling that our children were our responsibility.

"In light of the above, pressures mounted. My own efforts became less productive and my strength quickly weakened. My early academic skills were not producing the same results. I was losing the battle. I then recognized that I needed to give my work to the Lord and submit to the Holy Spirit. This occurred in three specific areas as I began each assignment: concept, process, and outcome. The enormous burden - overwhelming defeat - lifted and grades improved with each paper. God's will, not mine, directed my studies. I ended up getting an A in the course most challenging to me!"

Another student approached me. Her comment was, "When I heard what you said, something in me just broke. I don't know what it was, but I haven't been the same since that chapel."

Through my seeking God, and His revealing himself to me, I discovered something better than achievement: fulfillment.

Seeing those two students' lives changed made all my struggle and toil worth far more than a high grade. Eternal change took place in their lives. God's word was yielding seed for the sower (me) and bread for the eater (other students). I was beginning to feel God's pleasure, and wanted even more of that sweet taste to my soul. The thought that God would use me to bless other people was overwhelming. His transformation of my heart and motives was still in the making. My enrollment in the class of the heart was to be an ongoing prerequisite to His supernatural enablement.

I wondered what would follow next.

CHAPTER TEN

JOY AND PEACE

"You will go out in joy and be led forth in peace; the mountains and hills will burst into song before you, and all the trees will clap their hands."
(Isaiah 55:12)

Many times we think our purpose for going to school is primarily for an education. When we arrive and go through a little fire, we find that God has some other priorities in mind, too. As if it isn't enough for us to develop our minds, God puts us in His own spiritual "washing machine" at the same time. After about three cycles on heavy soil, He wrings us out and tosses us in the dryer... on hot!

His intention isn't to be mean to us. Rather, it is His aim for us to come out of school with a developed mind and a clean heart. In other words, He wants our experience to yield the fruit of joy and peace in our emotions, as well as for our experience to yield the fruit of a mind that can think critically and clearly.

People used to joke that CBNU didn't mean Christian Broadcasting Network University. It meant Christian Bootcamp, Not Utopia. God was in the business of training soldiers who would boldly take His love and truth into every marketplace in the world. Learning to walk by faith and love was just as important as learning to think. The Apostle Paul was a brilliant man, but he also wrote to the Corinthians that knowledge without love makes a man nothing.

43

God's deepest desire was to teach me His love, joy, and peace while I was in school, so that I could then give it to others. Although I didn't fully perceive His ultimate intention at the time, it has become evident to me that gently, but thoroughly, He was raining his love over every area of my life. Sometimes it was difficult to receive the spiritual nourishment He wanted to give because the soil of my heart was so hardened by independence.

When a child has a traumatic experience, such as the death of a parent at an early and critical age, that child will find some way to survive. When my father died, one of my modes of survival was to excel and achieve in school and in sports. Erecting thick, almost impenetrable walls of independence in my heart was a necessary defense system for my survival.

God was in the process of replacing my self-constructed defense system with His love. One of the ways He made that known to me was through the servanthood of another student.

During the summer quarter of 1984 I decided to do an independent study project. I wanted to produce my own video. Although I had no technical instruction, I didn't think it would be a problem to create the video and have some of my friends help me shoot it and edit it. The finished video was to be about ten minutes long.

By the time I finished preparing everything I wanted to include in the video, it ended up about thirty minutes in length. Most people thought that this was my graduate portfolio, but it was just a simple two credit assignment. I overextended myself once again, but I was fascinated with the creative process.

My friend Dino volunteered to help me edit the video. Little did I realize that editing a thirty minute video would require about thirty to fifty hours of Dino's time. Never once did he complain. In fact, he expressed nothing but a sincere desire to help me produce my video. My heart was so touched by his joyful servanthood. In a rare and lovely way, God was showing how much He loved me through Dino's unconditional loving way of assisting me.

During the timing of this project, I felt a strange pull in my heart one morning to pray. One of my favorite places to pray at the university was in the little chapel on the second floor of the library. Once there, I spent some time pouring out my heart to God: "Lord, I realize this morning that I have never submitted my emotions to Your lordship. I have willfully surrendered my academics (what I do with my mind) to You, but this area of my life is something that I have not fully turned over to Your control. Please take charge over my emotions. I want You to be Lord over every area of my life." With all sincerity and seriousness I offered up my petition. This must have been important to God, because He answered it just a few hours later.

Once the majority of the editing was finished, I was anxious to view the video. While watching it during my lunch break at work, the phone rang. As I swung myself around the desk to reach the phone, I hit the television monitor. After I hung up the phone, I glanced back at the screen. What was supposed to be a beach scene was a baseball player swinging a bat! Apparently I hit a wrong button on the television which recorded over my video. I just erased part of the master tape!

Normally I would totally freak out in a situation like this one. Unlike my typical normal response, I calmly reassured myself with a prayer, "Lord, earlier this morning I surrendered my emotions to You. You allowed this to happen. If I have to re-edit the entire video again, and if it takes just as long, I will do it." I couldn't believe how unaffected I was. No anger. No disgust at my mistake. I didn't want to find a bridge and jump off it. I just wanted to call Dino and find out what he could do. Unexplainable peace filled my heart.

After assessing the situation, Dino looked at me at said, "Veronica, I could patch up the video, but it will have a major glitch in it. I would like to do the whole thing over again. If we are going to do it, we are going to do it right. I want your video to be excellent."

What a friend! After thirty more hours of editing, the video was finally finished. Even more than the video representing excellent work was the excellence of spirit that Dino conveyed to me throughout the entire project. This precious student dedicated about eighty hours of his time to help me through thick and thin in my assignment. What a powerful demonstration of God's love for me! Dino's act of kindness towards me will remain fresh in my memory forever.

As a result of Dino's example to me, I found myself experiencing God's lordship of my emotions, especially in responding to unexpected happenings in my life. God was leading me forth with joy and peace in a new way. Although I had entered into situations with struggle and striving, He was leading me out of them with a vibrancy of spirit and a deeper level of trust in Him. God used Dino to reach out to me in selfless love. I wondered if I could share that love with other students.

CHAPTER ELEVEN

MORE FRUIT AND THE NEXT STEP

"Instead of the thornbush will grow the pine tree, and instead of briers the myrtle will grow. This will be for the Lord's renown, for an everlasting sign, which will not be destroyed." (Isaiah 55:13)

During the winter quarter of 1984, I finally saw some fruit on my vine. I was making great grades, but more importantly, I was beginning to realize the fruit of the Holy Spirit. What was once dry and filled with drudgery was now becoming a delight. His love, joy, peace, patience, etc., was with me in my studies. I was developing a deep love in my heart for the field of communication. Although I originally had chosen this major out of obedience, I was now enjoying the blessing of being obedient. God knew what He was doing even when I didn't fully understand His choice for me.

It was also during the winter quarter of 1984 that I saw some financial fruit on my vine. I was going through my course book deciding what classes I would choose for the spring term. My routine was to pray about each selection because I wanted to take the courses in line with God's will. I would not settle on a course selection until I had peace in my heart.

As I examined the communication course offerings, I decided to turn to the section on Biblical Studies. Another spur-of-the-moment thought entered my mind. Immediately, I offered it up to God: "Lord, look at all these Biblical Studies courses I will never be able to take. I wonder what it would be like to pursue another degree in Biblical Studies? If You make the way, I'll do it."

Two days later I received a call from the financial aid office. "Veronica, you have been awarded a Beazley scholarship worth $5,000." One of the stipulations for receiving the money was that the student could not have completed fifty percent of her degree program. The only way I could accept the scholarship was to pursue another degree. Not only did God confirm my desire to enter into the School of Biblical Studies, but He sponsored me upfront with money!

Following God in my studies was paying off! The Beazley scholarship was the most coveted financial award the university offered. More importantly, I knew that the $100 seed I had planted in Fayetteville before leaving for school had finally yielded a return. I felt the pleasure of God.

A degree in Biblical Studies would require another year and a half, making my total time at the university three years. I was in no hurry. My main objective was to know God. The timing of my life was His business. I was caught up in the middle of a divine adventure that I did not want to end. The richness of God's love, grace, and provision was sweet to my taste. I liked the fruit of following God and I was ready for the next step.

God further confirmed the next step in my life through a word from Terry, another student. In a written note, Terry expressed the following words of encouragement: "Veronica, I feel impressed that the Lord would say to you: 'I know your heart, my daughter. I know that you desire purity and my will. Rest assured and know that I am now preparing you for your next season in life. I have only good things for you. I have been with you through every struggle and have been faithful to your every need. Rest and know that I am in control. I have marvelous plans for you. Do not look to the circum-stances of the world. Rather, look beyond into the domain of My presence and peace. I love you with an everlasting love.'"

What was the next step? It was something more than adding on more courses to my academic record. It was to be something more than adding professional refinement for a career. It was to be the beginning of a ministry that would bear eternal fruit for the kingdom of God. My next communication class would provide the vehicle to begin sharing with other students who also needed the touch of God in their academic lives.

CHAPTER TWELVE

LEARNING ABILITY
VS. LEARNING CAPACITY

*"No eye has seen, no ear has heard, no mind has conceived what God
has prepared for those who love him' but God has revealed it to us
by his Spirit."* (1 Corinthians 2:9, 10)

Every now and then a student needs the total freedom to create
his own thoughts and develop his own biblical views in an academic
discipline. Communication Theory class provided this opportunity
for me. Our biggest assignment for the course was to develop our
own communication theory. We could do it on anything we wanted,
as long as it fulfilled the basic elements of communication between
the sender and receiver.

I was excited to develop a communication theory that would
articulate in a written way what I had been experiencing in my
studies with God. After studying the Bible for some time, I developed what I called "The From God - To God Theory of Study."

Instead of focusing on rational knowledge, the kind of knowledge
that is based on our five senses, I focused on revelation knowledge.
Revelation knowledge is the kind of knowledge that God reveals to
us through the Holy Spirit. It makes God our source of wisdom, not
our own minds.

The theory included four main propositions:

1. God is the source of all knowledge, insight, understanding, and wisdom.

   "Who has understood the mind of the Lord or instructed him as his counselor? Whom did the Lord consult to enlighten him, and who taught him the right way? Who was it that taught him knowledge or showed him the path of understanding?" (Isaiah 40:13-14)

   "To God belong wisdom and power; counsel and understanding are his." (Job 12:13)

2. God actively seeks to impart His wisdom and knowledge to us.

   "For the Lord gives wisdom, and from his mouth come knowledge and understanding." (Proverbs 2:6)

   "To you, 0 men, I [wisdom] callout; I raise my voice to all mankind." (Proverbs 8:4)

3. The key quality to receiving wisdom is humility and the fear of the Lord.

   "Trust in the Lord with all your heart and lean not on your own understanding; in all your ways acknowledge him, and he will make your paths straight. Do not be wise in your own eyes; fear the Lord and shun evil." (Proverbs 3:5-7)

   "The fear of the Lord teaches a man wisdom, and humility comes before honor." (Proverbs 15:33)

   "The fear of the Lord is the beginning of knowledge." (Proverbs 1:7)

   "If you callout for insight and cry aloud for understanding, and if you look for it as for silver and search for it as for hidden treasure, then you will...find the knowledge of God." (Proverbs 2:3-5)

4. God expects the credit for giving His knowledge and wisdom.

"From him and through him and to him are all things." (Romans 11:36)

"Everyone who is called by my name, whom I created for my glory, whom I formed and made." (Isaiah 43:7)

"I will not give my glory to another or my praise to idols." (Isaiah 42:8b)

The dynamic that made the model work was love. If the student did not believe that God loved him, then he could not receive from God. Also, if the student's motive was not to love God in return, then God could not get the glory.

The time came for each student to present his theory to the class. I drew a circle on the board, drew a smiley-faced God at the twelve o'clock position, a smiley-faced student at the six o'clock position, with arms outstretched to God, and began my explanation. Students listened intently, and looked at me with fresh interest. Afterwards, a few came up to me and expressed further interest in what I shared. It was a new concept to them, although the truths were age-old. Essentially, what I was attempting to get across to them was the difference between learning ability and learning capacity.

One student came up with the following insight regarding the difference between the two:

"I had a position paper to write for Dr. Cox's class. Four weeks ago I had a topic chosen and began researching when I came against a blank wall. After pounding on it for several days, I finally gathered that the topic I had chosen was not what God had chosen for me to do. I read through the list of *issue* questions. Our paper was to be written from one of the questions on this list. One jumped off the page: Does the Holy Spirit give us better learning abilities? I knew right then what the Lord wanted me to do.

"The research came together quickly, but when I sat down to write, nothing came. I couldn't understand it. I prayed about it, but still hit a wall. I began to weep and cry. There was something that the Lord wanted me to learn, and it wasn't coming through. I left it. The evening before I was going to turn the paper in, I was studying for a final. The Holy Spirit prompted me to pray for the other students in the class. As I began to pray for them, God began to speak to me about my paper. It was so exciting. What God had been trying to teach me was so simple. I wrote the paper with the anointing of the Spirit. Now let me share with you the gist of the paper.

"Noah Webster defines 'learning' as the gaining of knowledge or ideas previously unknown. 'Abilities' *is* defined as the active power to perform. The reason I could not write the paper before was because my perspective was not right. I believe that what God showed me was this: While the Holy Spirit *is* certainly capable of giving better learning ability, His much higher purpose is to give better learning *capacity*. Webster defines 'capacity' as the power to receive. Thus, learning capacity could be defined as the power to receive knowledge or ideas previously unknown. Instead of being performance-oriented. I needed to be oriented to receive knowledge from God! The Holy Spirit gives us better learning capacity."

God had revealed to this student the essence of what He had revealed to me: There are two kinds of knowledge: rational knowledge and revelation knowledge. The key to gaining revelation knowledge is receiving.

It became my prayer to learn how to receive better from God, so that I could more fully glorify Him in return. The fact of the matter is, it is ludicrous to thank someone for something you think you earned on your own. You only thank someone for something he assisted you with, or gave you freely. My Biblical Studies program would provide me with more ample opportunity *in* my holy investigations! But first, I would have another unexpected happening. It would come as a praise from a professor.

CHAPTER THIRTEEN

UNEXPECTED PRAISE FOR LOVING GOD

"Love the Lord your God...with all your mind" (Matthew 22:37).

My next acting class was TV Drama. Dr. Shouse was once again my professor. My assignment was to play a hard-to-get girl at a dance. (That was an easy assignment!) I also had to play an old Italian woman for the script "Marty." At the same time, I was the head costume director.

I was so used to studying independently that it was a real joy to feel part of a team. No production could take place without each person doing his part. I liked that. Although it was quite a task to find 1950's clothes for each member of the cast, I set out to do my part with joy.

The production was a success and the day came for the class critique. When it was my turn, Dr. Shouse warmly smiled and said, "You are a hallmark student, an example to others and to me. I have gained a tremendous amount of respect for you this semester. Despite the challenge of your task as the costume director, you went about your task with joy. I can't imagine God not honoring your efforts. He has to."

I was deeply honored and humbled. In fact, I felt a bit embarrassed because I did not expect such a high compliment. But God used it to show me that when we do our work to please Him, others are blessed in the process. Dr. Shouse's comments were an unexpected confirmation to me of this principle of blessing. Her praise motivated me all the more to glorify God in my studies.

If teachers only realized what a tremendous source of inspiration they can be to their students, I think they would be more motivated in their teaching, and see greater results in their students' learning. If students only knew what it meant to a teacher to see a wholehearted effort, they might find it more satisfying to give it their best shot. Nowadays, it seems that so much education is impersonal. Computers take the place of instructors. The heart of learning has been replaced with a hard drive. The magic of relationship between a student and teacher has become a rare experience.

Dr. Shouse's comment to me was important enough for me to write it down in my journal. It edified me, inspired me, and made me appreciate her all the more as someone who truly cared about building me up. It also made me want to try even harder.

God himself desires this kind of wholehearted relationship. The greatest commandment says it best: "Love the Lord your God with all your heart and with all your soul and with all your mind." As we love God with our hearts and souls and minds as students, then the second commandment will be fulfilled, "Love your neighbor as yourself" (Matthew 22:37-39). Loving our fellow students and our teacher *is* a higher aim and builds a more eternal foundation to our work than merely performing an academic task.

The command to love God with our minds means that studying is a holy pursuit. If what we do with our minds is mainly study, then we are challenged to make our studying an offering worthy of His praise. There is no longer a dividing line between the secular and the sacred. In Jesus all our studies become a sacred pursuit. Whether we are studying the Bible or economics, the issue is: what is the attitude of your heart? Whether you are teaching the Bible or economics, it's still the same issue: what is the attitude of your heart?

CHAPTER FOURTEEN

"I WANT MY A, GOD!"

"Let us then approach the throne of grace with confidence, so that we may receive mercy and find grace to help us in our time of need"
(Hebrews 4:16).

My first class in Biblical Studies was Principles of Bible Study. Excited to start my new course of study, I told my friend about it. "Oh my, you're taking that class with that professor? Don't you know that he's the terror of the Biblical Studies department? I made a C in that class, and you will, too," was her comment.

"Oh, yeah?" I thought to myself. "How dare she make such a comment!" That night I said to the Lord, "God, the fact of the matter is, I don't know a thing about Biblical Studies. I haven't even read through the whole Old Testament. I may be a novice at this, but You're not. You wrote the book! I may be insufficient in this class, but You are sufficient. I may be ignorant, but You know everything! Besides, I'm your daughter, and I expect You to help me. I am making a commitment to You to give everything I have to this class, because I don't want a C. I want my A!"

My prayer continued, "Lord, if You really are the Source of all wisdom and knowledge, and if I have access to You, then why can't I make straight A's through two master's programs? The glory would go to You. I wonder if You will commit yourself to me in this divine project? I wonder what You would do if I were faithful and diligent?

Although I am capable of making good grades on my own, I know that I am not capable of a 4.0 G.P.A through two master's. That would have to be a work of your grace, favor, and intelligence working through me." I made it my aim to make a 4.0 G.P.A through both of my graduate degrees. I was curious to see how God would respond to my request. After all, He did it for Daniel. Would He do it for me?

Principles of Bible Study was a bear of a class. The professor was extremely detailed, and expected us to work very hard, but he graded us fairly. The last assignment was worth twenty percent of the grade. After I completed it, I knew it wasn't good enough to make an A. Have you ever done an assignment, gave it everything you had, and knew it still didn't cut it? No matter how I tried to doctor it up, nothing worked. This time I prayed a prayer I never prayed before in my studies. "Lord, I pray for Your mercy. Your word says that You hold the heart of every king in your hand. You must hold the heart of every professor in Your hand, too. Please grant me Your mercy in this assignment."

When I got the assignment back, I looked very closely at the grade. To my recollection, the professor never graded in pencil. Looking at my paper, I saw that he wrote down one grade and erased it to a higher grade. Then he erased that, and wrote down an even higher grade. I got my A! The professor changed my grade twice! Obviously God had answered my prayer for mercy! I got an A in my first Biblical Studies course! More importantly, I saw God's faithfulness to me again, this time in a whole new dimension of His character. I wondered what was next.

CHAPTER FIFTEEN

AN UNEXPECTED VISITOR AT STUDY TIME

"Now this is eternal life: that they may know you, the only true God, and Jesus Christ, whom you have sent" (John 17:3).

In my Principles of Bible Study class God revealed to me His mercy. In my next class, God would unexpectedly reveal another facet of His glorious nature.

I loved all of my "God, the World, and Man" theology classes. You didn't just attend these classes. You experienced God in them. For ten weeks I would absorb myself with the truths of God's character, His eternal plan for man, how man messed things up, and how God redeemed man's mess. This would be my first systematic study. Although I looked forward to every class with eager expectation, I think God looked forward to my continued learning of Him even more.

Each class would begin with prayer and praise. The presence of God permeated the room. What an atmosphere for learning! As our minds were attuned to the truths of God, our spirits were opened so God could sink those truths home to us personally in our hearts.

It was during this course that God did a heavy duty renewal of my mind as to who He really was in my life. It is common knowledge that the image we have of our earthly father is the same image we construct of our heavenly Father. If we perceive our earthly father to be kind, loving, and out for our best interests, that is how we will view God. If we see our earthly father as harsh, unforgiving, and a stern disciplinarian, that is how we will view our heavenly Father.

I knew my earthly father loved me, but he rarely expressed that love to me verbally. He also worked very hard to provide for us, so he spent little time entering into my world as a child. In our strict Catholic home, I learned early that black was black and white was white. There was very little in between. Furthermore, there certainly wasn't any room for us kids to express our emotions as people. What Daddy said was right. Period. The religious mentality I was instilled with also bred in me a mentality of suffering. As such, life was something that one suffers through. Work was the enemy that kept my father from spending time with me.

Although my religious upbringing instilled in me a deep reverence for God, my concept of God was still warped. In my spirit, I saw God as a stern disciplinarian who was ready to hit me over the head with His holy hammer any time I made a mistake. He certainly was not someone who played or worked with me. He had his own thing to do. Moreover, I certainly was not free to approach God with any sense that my feelings were valid, because they did not mean anything, or so I thought. Why would God want to spend time with me? He was too busy working, keeping the world in order.

My father's death when I was fifteen years old had complicated things. If my own father left me, why wouldn't God leave me, too? Of course, these thoughts were not conscious, but they did form my view of God.

It was as if God were working overtime to disprove my faulty notions of who He was. He put me in school where I was inundated with the truth of who He was from a scholarly viewpoint. Then He put me in the home of the school's head counselor. As if it weren't enough to get counseling once a week, I was confronted with a personal counselor as my roommate! Then in my own personal quest in my studies God was showing up on the scene in a mighty way. Studying for my theology midterm was no exception.

The morning of preparing for the exam was a difficult one. I did not want to study! How do you psyche yourself up to do something that in the flesh you don't want to do? You use your imagination!

If I had to study, I was going to create an enjoyable environment. I moved my dining room table to the living room, so the courtyard could be in my view. Then I turned on some classical music to stimulate my mind. Taking out my books, I prayed and offered up the time to God.

In the third hour of studying for the exam, something happened which has not occurred again to this day. If was as if I was taken into another realm. My study time was literally transformed into a worship time. The Holy Spirit invaded my living room. Tears began to stream down my face. God unexpectedly decided to visit me during my study time. I was having a face-to-face encounter with the living God.

God began to reveal to me His eternal nature. It was a new, deeper understanding that when time ceases to be, I'm going to be with Him. He will never leave my presence, and I will never leave His. When that day comes, I will never again have any tinge of fear that God is going to leave me, even for a split second.

The revelation lasted about five minutes. I wanted it to last longer, but for those few moments of time, I was caught up in another world. This was an incredibly significant truth God revealed to me. He wanted me to know that even though my earthly father left me, my heavenly Father would never leave me. I would be with Him forever. Something deep inside me was healed forever, too. And it all happened as I was preparing for an exam.

How about you? Do you know that God's love for you is from

everlasting to everlasting? Maybe you are a Christian, but you still doubt the Father's love for you, as I did. If you do, why don't you stop right now and ask God to reveal His love to you? Confess your fear. Tell Him what's on your heart.

Someone once said to me, "Veronica, God loves you. You are the apple of his eye. He will never leave you or forsake you. It's time you start believing it for yourself!" That shook me up! Maybe it's time you start believing for yourself that God loves *you*.

CHAPTER SIXTEEN

DIVINE ENTHUSIASM AND THE SEARCH FOR GOLDEN NUGGETS

"And without faith it is impossible to please God, because anyone who comes to him must believe that he exists and that he rewards those who earnestly seek him." (Hebrews 11:6).

Where does the enthusiasm to study come from?

One of the greatest problems facing students is motivation. Some study because they are interested in the subject. Others study because their parents pressure them. Scholarships and future job opportunities can be motivating factors. Desire to be knowledgeable in a certain subject can move one to study. The list goes on.

It's not that any of the above motives are wrong in and of themselves. They are simply not enough to keep a student motivated when pressures mount or other priorities compete for time. Also, the above motivations to study do not payoff in immediate rewards.

When the "study stealers" come, they speak with a powerful voice. You recognize the way they talk: "You can do this tomorrow. Your favorite television show is on. Sally Stupendous Student hasn't started her assignment yet. You don't have to start yours either. School is supposed to be a party. Others won't like you if you appear too committed. Blow it off if you want to be cool. Just do what's necessary to get it done. You don't have to do your best. What good is this trigonometry going to do five years from now?"

In the beginning, God created man to have fellowship with Him. In the Garden, God brought all His creatures to Adam to name. Can you imagine if you were Adam? God comes to you and says, "Adam, I am going to give you an assignment. I would like you to name all the birds of the air and all the beasts of the field" (Genesis 2:19,20). Would you freak out? Would the task be too overwhelming for you? Would you think about being motivated by future job opportunities? Maybe God would promote you to head VP of Titles. Would you think about pulling any name out of the hat just to complete the assignment? Would you tell God that you were just too busy watching MTV? How would you respond?

After all, the Creator of the Universe has just let you in on His handiwork. He has initiated the assignment. Perhaps, just maybe, consider the possibility, that this was something that God looked forward to Himself. That is, a time whereby God would include Adam in the work of His creation. A time for God and Adam to meet together over a study session. Could God have intended learning to be a partnership with Him? Is that really too outrageous of a proposition?

Consider my point from a human perspective. What if Oprah called you on the phone and wanted to help you with your media career? What if Michael Jordon walked up to you on the basketball court and offered to help you with your lay up shot? What if Tom Hanks asked to assist you in your acting? What then would be your motivation?

You would do it screaming with energy, not so much because of what you were doing, but with whom you were doing it! The motivation would not be coming from you, or from the activity, but from another person.

One time when I was playing golf, I had the opportunity to play with one of the greatest senior amateurs of all time. Struggling with some health problems, he did not play very well. However, the effect he had on my game was nothing but positive. I was playing with a great champion, and I knew it! The mere fact that it was a high privilege to be in his presence motivated me to play well. The same holds true with academics.

Who do you think is responsible for the knowledge behind the subject area you are studying? Ecclesiastes 12:11 says, "The words of the wise are like prodding goads, and firmly fixed (in the mind) like nails are the collected sayings which are given (as proceeding) from one Shepherd" (AMP). That Shepherd is God. He created the universe and everything in it. He is your heavenly Father and wants to study with you! How much more motivation do you need?

The word "enthusiasm" comes from the Latin words "en theos," meaning "in God". *Webster's New Collegiate Dictionary* defines enthusiasm as "belief in special revelations of the Holy Spirit." In other words, to be enthused about something is to be inspired by God. Enthusiasm is a feeling of excitement, zeal, or passion that is a result of receiving inspiration from God.

I believe that in the beginning, before sin came into the world, that God Himself was the Source of man's motivation. Working, studying, and learning in His presence was man's highest energizing force. It was the communication between God and man that fueled man's daily activity. When sin entered the world, man became self-centered in his motivations, and lost his "en theos," his enthusiasm.

Consider another analogy from a human perspective. One time I was riding in a car with one of my brother's friends in North Carolina. I wasn't thrilled about the four-hour ride. "This is going to be boring," I thought. "It's bad enough that I'm not traveling with someone whom I know. I can't even play my favorite music tapes. I'm sure he's not into Christian music."

The ride turned out to be one of the most enjoyable rides I can remember. We had a marvelous conversation. The time flew by. Although we had very little in common, I discovered he was a Christian. We encouraged one another. I hadn't been looking forward to making a four-hour trip, but I loved the conversation so much that it made the trip worthwhile and meaningful.

If one person had done all the talking, the trip would have been boring to me. If all we did was listen to music, the trip would have been dry. It was the interaction that made all the difference.

In your academic ride, are you engaging in a conversation with God? Have you ever recognized that He is seated in the vehicle with you? Do you know that He is looking forward to taking this trip with you? (After all, He is responsible for the ride in the first place!) And have you offered to let *Him* drive?

When I made God my Study Buddy, the person with whom I would travel through my academics, the ride became exciting.

Friday nights would be special study nights. As I entered into the library with my stack of books, people would give me strange looks and say, "Veronica, you're going to study on a Friday night?" And although many students would view a Friday night in the library as drudgery, my new outlook transformed these times into opportunities for fresh revelation. I could honestly say, "God is going to teach me something tonight and I don't want to miss out!"

Before I would begin to study, I would lay my hands on my books and pray, "Father, I expect You to teach me something tonight. My expectation to learn is of You. I am not trusting in the book to be my teacher. I am expecting You to teach me something about the subject matter, Your character, or something about me."

Every time I sat down to study, I would expect God to reveal a golden nugget of truth to me about something. It would be up to Him to decide what that would be. Sometimes I would gain some insight into the subject area I was studying. Other times I would get a deep sense of His faithfulness in being with me. Still other times, I would feel a strengthening of my character as I became more diligent in my studies.

It is not wrong to expect God to reward you for your diligence. In fact, God is the Ultimate Rewarder. The Bible says that you must have faith to believe Him for who He is. When you diligently seek Him, He will reward you. (Read Hebrews 11:6.) The perspective I developed in my studies was one of a divine adventure. I sought God diligently in my studies. It was up to Him to decide how to reward me. Friday nights became my "treasure hunt" nights. God would do the hiding of the golden nuggets and I would do the hunting until I came upon the finding!

Some of you who like to hunt, whether it is for animals or for bargains, I challenge you to start hunting for God's treasures of wisdom and knowledge! It paid off for me. How do you begin your golden nugget search? The answer is simpler than you might think.

CHAPTER SEVENTEEN

THE WAY TO GOD'S FAVOR

"You have been faithful with a few things; I will put you in charge of many things." (Matthew 25:23).

In the parable of the talents, three servants were given three different amounts of money, each according to his ability. The first two went out, invested their money, and earned a profit. The third, however, was afraid of his master. Unlike the other two, he dug a hole and hid his money in the ground.

When the master returned from his journey, he went to settle accounts with his servants. Because the first two yielded a return on their investment, they were rewarded with greater charge over the master's property. The third servant was cast out of his master's household and called wicked, lazy, and worthless (Matt. 25:26, 30). The master also took away his one talent and gave it to the most productive servant.

The bottom line lesson of this story is that God expects His servants to be productive in His kingdom! The key quality to productivity in God's economy is faithfulness. Ultimately, I'm talking about faithfulness to the Master, not to mere performance.

Faithfulness to God in the little things will transform your academic life. For instance, many students have trouble getting to class on time, turning papers in on time, or proofreading their papers. These are little, but significant disciplines. Perhaps their

69

attitude is, "Who cares if I'm late? So what if I'm docked five points on my paper for turning it in late. It's no big deal. Proofreading? The teacher ought to be glad I wrote the paper in the first place. I don't have time to scrutinize my work."

In God's economy, that kind of attitude is disastrous because God cannot reward carelessness. Furthermore, that kind of self-centeredness is an insult to God. It's as if the student credits God for the opportunity to be in school and then acts like he could care less in the process of his education. God is worthy of our best in every situation, small or big.

Another insight from the story of the talents is that God looks at people individually. He did not expect each servant to perform equally. Each one was expected to produce a return according to his own ability.

Let's face it. Not everyone is gifted to study. For some, it takes a long time to read. For others math is a bear. God does not expect a married person with four kids to be able to spend the same amount of time as a single person with less responsibility. Students could enjoy much greater freedom if they quit comparing themselves to others and allow their standard of performance to be determined by their own level of faithfulness to God.

Personally, I decided to be faithful to God in the small things because I believed that in honoring Him wherever I could, He would honor me with His grace and favor in those crunch times when I really needed it. Therefore, I was always sure to attend class on time and turn in papers when they were due. In fact, I never missed a class during finals time. I trusted that if I were faithful to God in my studies, then I would have all the time I needed to prepare for my exams.

Are you catching my drift? I took what was dutiful and turned it into a covenant commitment to God. If I was faithful to do my best, then I could expect God to return His best to me. Again, if I were faithful in the small things, I could expect God to be faithful in rewarding me with bigger things. The small tasks became the most significant to me because they were a way to find God's favor and blessing.

The normal routine of study and attending class became daily divine appointments with God. What can you do to turn the mundane into an act of eternal significance? You can turn what you don't want to do into an act of faithfulness to God. You can show up on time with the expectation that God will reward you. I wonder what would happen to you if you did.

I remember one student in graduate school who wanted to be a great evangelist. Granted, he was gifted with the ability to preach and persuade people. But he never came to class! He wanted to go out and conquer the world without submitting to the disciplines of training. It became a class joke to see if he would show up or not. I felt sorry for him because I knew that God could not bless him with the big things. He was not faithful in the little things.

Sometimes God may interrupt your study time to show you something more important. In my own study walk, I remember there were times when being faithful to God in my studies meant not studying. God knew me better than I knew myself. Sometimes He would impress on my spirit that I needed to put my books down and go out and play. Other times, He would lead me away from my studies to teach me something else.

One time I was studying for finals. God impressed upon my heart to lay everything aside and attend some special services at church. "But God, you know I'm studying for tests. What's the deal?" I felt like God said, "Trust me and go. I'll take care of your finals." I'm glad I obeyed because God wanted to minister to me in another area of my life. As a result of those meetings, I received inner healing from some things that had been holding me back spiritually and emotionally. Praise God! You can trust Him to schedule your life.

In short, be faithful to God. Write out a covenant agreement with God if you want. Follow your own fingerprints. You are an individual and God created you that way. Don't get into bondage trying to keep up with your classmates in your studies. Simply live up to God's standards for you. Be consistent in the small things and expect Him to reward you with greater things. He did this for me and will do it for you, too. He loves you!

CHAPTER EIGHTEEN

WRITING FROM MY HEART

"Faith by itself, if it is not accompanied by action, is dead." (James 2:17)

Writing is difficult for me. Every paper I wrote in graduate school required great effort and struggle. Some people can wait until the last minute to write a paper. I couldn't. So many times I would think great thoughts. But transferring those thoughts from my head to paper was like crossing the Atlantic Ocean during an airline strike. In a rowboat, no less.

Fortunately, I was fairly disciplined by this time to take my study frustrations to the Lord. "God, there has to be an easier way to go about writing. Please send help."

It wasn't long before the Lord sent me a friend to coach me in my writing. His name was Dominic. As a professional writer and graduate of the university, he sympathized with my situation. After classes I would visit with Dom and we would discuss my paper topics.

"Veronica, what do you want to say?" he would ask me. I would reply, "This is what I want to say..." and spout off a volume full of thoughts. He would smile and say, "Good, now write it down," as though that settled everything. Except that at this point, I would freeze up. Sheepishly looking at Dom, I had to admit, "I can't remember what I said."

This kind of interaction happened time after time. Finally, during one session, Dom looked at me like a light bulb had just gone on over his head and said, "You know what your problem is? You don't believe that writing from your heart is good enough, do you?"

He was right. It was good enough for me to think something, but the moment I had to transfer my thoughts to paper, my simple words weren't enough. I thought I had to make my words more intellectual. Words like "green" and "school" in my mind had to become "verdant" and "institution" on the written page.

"Trash that kind of thinking," he told me. Then he gave me a terrific piece of advice that became my guideline for writing: "Write your heart and write it just as you would speak it. Keep it simple and don't try to intellectualize it." It was a new way of approaching things and it set me free.

The other problem I had was the way I went about writing a paper. First I would pick a topic. Then I would take out ten to twenty books and research what everybody else said about the subject. Afterwards, I would spend the next three weeks trying to figure out a way to blend together what everyone had to say on the subject. Of course I would add my own introduction and conclusion.

My intention was that the paper would turn out like a mosaic. Instead, it turned out like a bunch of ingredients thrown into the blender. It came out like a milkshake with no distinct flavor. No wonder I was struggling and bored with writing papers.

Dom's input set me straight. I realized that papers could be the result of my own creative process. I could use research to support or oppose my thoughts, rather than to take the place of them. Not only did Dom show me that my thoughts were valid, but he challenged me to have faith in writing what was on my heart. After all, the heart is the place where the Holy Spirit speaks to us and through us. If I was afraid to write from my heart, I was quenching the Holy Spirit.

Writing from my heart was indeed a step of faith for me. I knew how to get a good grade, but this kind of thinking put me in a whole new dimension of study. I was now vulnerable. No longer would I be in control of the outcome.

I had the chance to take another step of faith in my studies in Dr. Rea's class. We were given the assignment of writing a paper on anything from Genesis to Joshua. Reading through the Bible, I came across Genesis 6:5,6: "The Lord saw how great man's wickedness on the earth had become, and that every inclination of the thoughts of his heart was only evil all the time. The Lord was grieved that he had made man on the earth, and his heart was filled with pain."

This was the first time in the Bible since the creation of the world that God expressed His heart. He was sorry that He had made man. What a concept -- to think of a God who expresses remorse! No matter how I tried to read on, I kept coming back to this passage. It pricked my heart. Obviously, the Holy Spirit was leading me to write on the subject, "Out of the Broken Heart of God." He gave me the title and the scripture. Now all I had to do was write the paper. I was off and running. It was an exciting feeling to hear my spirit speaking to me and to respond accordingly.

My weekend was dedicated to the writing of my paper. I still struggled! Ugh! After finally finishing it, I took it to Dom to read. He paged through it and said, "Veronica, this stinks! You need to write this over again." Shocked at his reaction, I shot back, "I'm not going to write anything over again. How can you say that? I spent this whole weekend slaving over this thing! Besides, it's due tomorrow." Undaunted by all my squealing and squawking, Dom continued to nail me: "Do you know what you did here? You didn't think that if you wrote from your heart that you would have enough to fill up the ten-page requirement. So instead, you wrote eight pages of filler. Isn't that right?" He had me figured out. Feeling exasperated and a tad guilty, I finally gave in and said, "Yes. Okay, Dom. I'll write the paper over."

Before I left his office, we wrote down a simple formula for writing papers from the heart:

1. Read. Do assignment. Do research. Take notes.

2. Pray.

3. Ask yourself, "What do I want to say?" (You may want to ask a friend to ask you the question.) Do the outline.

4. Say it. Write it down just like you said it.

5. As you're saying it, places will come to plug in references.

6. When it is done, ask yourself what finishing touches it needs.

I took the formula home. That evening I sat down and cried. "Jesus, please help me rewrite this paper. Forgive me for not doing this right from the start. I don't have a lot of time, so please let the words and organization flow." My Study Buddy responded immediately.

CHAPTER NINETEEN

BLESSING MY PROFESSOR

"We continually remember before our God and Father your work produced by faith, your labor prompted by love, and your endurance inspired by hope in our Lord Jesus Christ." (1 Thessalonians 1:3)

As I began to rewrite the paper, the words and ideas started coming so fast, I had trouble writing it all down. Dom stopped by and made some helpful suggestions.

After it was all through I cried again! Unlike the tears earlier in the day, these were tears of joy. My paper was fantastic! This was the first time I ever liked a paper I wrote. I did it! I wrote my first paper from the heart. At that moment I didn't care what grade I got. The important thing was that I was obedient to the leading of the Lord.

I must confess that deciding to write my paper from the heart was a profound act of faith on my part. This paper represented the first time I leaned solely on the Lord in concept, process, and outcome. It was like I was at the edge of a cliff. The only way for me to reach my Holy Grail in my studies was to jump off the cliff. What was awaiting me - a bridge or a fall to death - was not for me to know. I had to make the step before I would discover my fate.

Writing papers from the heart became a revolutionary way to go about my studies. The process began with prayer and listening to the leading of the Lord. It would not begin with my choosing topics based on what was easiest, safest, or what would naturally get the best response from the professor. It would mean writing in obedience to God and what He placed on my heart.

Before I handed it in, Dom reminded me of one of the most important elements of writing my paper, "Be sure to bless your professor, Veronica." Another revolutionary thought! I was learning how to love God in my studies and to minister to others. Blessing my professor added yet another dimension to my desire to integrate faith, love, and learning.

Blessing my professor could mean many things. In addition to reading a well-written term paper, it would bless him not to have to put any red correction marks on my paper. So I proofread my paper not once, like I normally did, but four or five times. I also prayed, "Lord, please let this paper be a blessing to Dr. Rea. In fact, I pray it so blesses his socks off that it brings a tear to his eye." With that, I turned in my paper.

It was a few weeks before I received my paper back. During that time, I was scared. The grade demons began to haunt me again. "You're not going to get a good grade. He's not going to like it. You'll be sorry..."

When I received the paper back, I was the one who was blessed! Dr. Rea gave me the highest grade I ever received from him on a paper. He even asked me for a copy of it! God answered my prayer. But that was not the end of the story.

I walked into a friend's office to give her a copy of my paper. There was a man standing next to her whom I did not know. A few weeks later I visited the network chapel. A lady came over to me and said, "I read a copy of your paper and loved it!" I thought to myself, "How in the world did this lady get a copy of my paper? I don't know her."

A few weeks later I visited the network chapel again and saw the same lady. With my curiosity getting the best of me, I walked over to her. "Can you please tell me how you got a copy of my paper?" I asked. The man standing next to her replied, "I can answer that. I was the man standing next to the friend to whom you gave the paper. She gave me a copy. I was so blessed by the paper that I ran a copy of it to everyone in my department!"

The story I was told was that this man had suffered through a divorce. He could not receive healing because he did not know that God could empathize with his pain. When he read this purely academic paper, God deeply touched his heart, and he received a healing from his divorce. Praise God!

All I wanted to do was bless my professor. God used my paper to bless more than one person! To see ministry take place as a result of doing an assignment gave me a whole new meaning to endnotes and footnotes! God used an academic paper for His glory. He took what I prepared through prayer, faith, love, and much thinking to further His kingdom. Writing my paper from the heart paid off in more than grades. It paid off with eternal dividends. It brought life.

My experience in writing Dr. Rea's paper from the heart remind-ed me of Jesus' parable about the kingdom,

"What shall we say the kingdom of God is like...? It is like a mustard seed, which is the smallest seed you plant in the ground. Yet when planted, it grows and becomes the largest of all garden plants, with such big branches that the birds of the air can perch in its shade." (Mark 4:30-32)

God took my mustard seed desire to bless my professor and multiplied it into a blessing beyond my imagination. He caused my labor of faith and love to grow into a tree where others could come and find some shade. Such is the Kingdom of God. I liked what was happening and wanted to experience more of the kingdom of God in my studies. The upcoming exam week provided me with such an opportunity.

CHAPTER TWENTY

HONORING GOD ON THE SABBATH

"A son honors his father, and a servant his master. If I am a father, where is the honor due me? If I am a master, where is the respect due me?" says the Lord." (Malachi 1:6)

One main reason the book of Malachi was written was to reprove priests for their unfaithfulness and lack of wholehearted service unto God. Instead of bringing unblemished sacrifices to the altar, the priests were offering crippled or diseased animals. They were not honoring God's name, nor were they giving proper and true instruction to the people. In short, God was mad at His servants! God was a great God and His name was worthy of praise. The half-hearted, mediocre, perfunctory service offered by the priests was not worthy of His name.

More than anything in my studies, I wanted to honor God. I didn't want to offer Him a meager effort when my best was what He deserved. At the same time, I found myself continuing to struggle with performance-orientation. Was I seeking God and His blessing because I wanted to know Him? Or was I seeking God because I wanted great grades? Every now and then I found myself still too caught up in my studies. The fact that I studied on Sundays began to bother me. God rested one day from His work during the week. Wouldn't it honor Him to follow His way of operating?

I felt like my studying on Sunday meant that I was honoring my grades more than I was honoring God. Was I willing to make a lower grade if it meant giving to God the time He deserved? Maybe for some, observing a Sabbath day rest is not an issue. For me it was. Exam week was the following week. What was I going to do?

I prayed, "Jesus, I want to honor You above all else. I have always studied on Sundays without any conviction that it was wrong. Now I feel like I want to take another step of faith and not study on this day of rest. You know that I have three major finals in just a few days. If I make lower grades because I am choosing to honor You on this day, I accept that. I trust you, God."

Sunday came and I did not study. I went to church, read my Bible and watched football on television. Around 4:00 pm the study demons began to speak into my ear, "What are you doing not studying? You're wasting precious time. That was a stupid decision."

I kept my promise, not knowing what God would do. I would find out early Monday morning how He would respond.

CHAPTER TWENTY-ONE

OVERWHELMING VICTORY THROUGH JOY POWER

"To the pure you show yourself pure. You give me your shield of victory. He holds victory in store for the upright. He is a shield to those whose walk is blameless." (Psalm 18:26a, 35a; Proverbs 2:7)

Monday morning I woke up with great joy! Usually I rolled out of bed, taking a while to feel like I was alive. In the morning I usually felt like a radio without batteries—no power. This morning, however, I awoke feeling like I had been on supercharge all night.

The Bible says that the joy of the Lord is my strength. It would be this supernatural joy that would be my missile power to get me through the week. What amazed me most was that I did not have to Bible-read it up, praise it up, or make a million confessions of my faith. I simply woke up with God's joy.

My joy continued to mount as specific scriptures hit home in my heart during my devotional time. In Psalm 18, David praises God for giving him overwhelming victory over all his foes, especially Saul. He rejoices that God has shown Himself faithful to the faithful. David rejoices that God's power enabled him to advance against a troop, scale a wall, run with the swiftness and agility of a deer, stand on the heights, train his hands for battle, and pursue, crush, and beat his enemies as fine as dust! I call that total victory!

God drew David out of deep waters and rescued him from his enemies who were too strong for him (vss. 16, 17). I felt God's deep assurance that He was going to do the same for me during my upcoming exam week. "You may be weak, Veronica, but I'm giving you the power of joy to give you total victory this week. Watch Me and see."

Because I honored God on Sunday, He honored me on Monday, Tuesday, and the rest of the week with supernatural enablement to crush all my study foes with total victory. My journal reflections summed up my experience: "I have never studied so hard in my life. For about one week I studied from eight to ten hours a day. I was sustained by the power of God! Never once did I feel burdened. The workload was tremendous, but I was able to advance against a troop and scale every wall!"

On my way to my first test I prayed, "Holy Spirit, I have prepared the best I could. Please don't let me forget to study anything important." Fifteen minutes before the test I ran into a friend of mine who was also taking the test. He was intensely studying a certain section of the textbook. "What are you studying?" I asked. It turned out that he was studying a chapter I had completely forgotten to study! I thought to myself, "Thank you, Holy Spirit, for answering my prayer."

In the remaining few minutes before the test I was able to brush up on the information. It was a good thing I took those few minutes to read it over, because it ended up being a major test question.

On another part of the test I forgot the answer. Knowing I had studied the information, I didn't panic. Instead, I stopped and calmly prayed, "Holy Spirit, please bring back to my remembrance what I studied." Within a few moments, I had my answer!

The Holy Spirit was right there with me, helping me to take my test! All I had to do was be faithful to study and depend upon His help.

In my next exam, I also experienced the presence and power of

God. Studying for this particular professor's exams was always a challenge. He had given us a three-page, single-spaced review sheet. It seemed like every subject known to man was on that sheet. I carefully reviewed the study sheet. However, once I looked over the exam, I realized that I had forgotten to review one of the subjects. Unfortunately, he made it a point to include it as a major essay question.

The question had to do with the concept of the divine warrior in the Old Testament. I wrote my answer, but with five minutes left in the exam time, I knew that I hadn't answered the question in the exact way in which he asked it. Nor could I figure out any way to change what I had written. Deciding to approach the professor about it, I showed him my paper and said, "This is how I answered the question. Is that okay?" He answered, "It's possible that you could answer it that way, but if it's wrong, it's wrong." Having peace in my heart, I turned it in. I left the class hanging onto the words I overheard from another student, "The victory is ours and the battle is the Lord's."

That night I had to study for my third final. Part of my Greek and Hebrew final was a take-home test. My constant prayer was, "Holy Spirit, please show me how to do this. Please show me if I am headed in the right direction with my answers."

I spent many hours researching and writing my answers. The following morning, a few hours before I turned in my exam, I was looking up an answer to another question. As I did that, I accidentally came across some information that showed me my first answer was all wrong. Immediately, I changed my answer. The Holy Spirit had answered my prayer again. I truly could depend upon God in the details of my academics. More importantly, the communion and growing trust in Him as my Lord was richer to me than any outstanding exam grade.

Whew! I had made it through the week. Once it was all over, I went back to the Lord. I especially wanted to talk to Him about the question I had on my first exam. "Lord, I couldn't believe that I forgot to study that particular subject on the divine warrior. Why did that happen?" I felt in my heart that God's answer was, "Veronica, that happened because I wanted to show you that I want to be your divine warrior. Your battles are my battles, whether they concern school or any other area of your life. You don't have to have all the answers. Where do you think your desire for excellence comes from? I told you I was going to give you the victory this week, and that is exactly what I am going to do."

Sometimes it is easy for us to believe we are sinners and that we need to repent when we sin. Maybe it's a little harder to believe in the flip side of who we are -- cleansed, washed in the blood, and totally victorious in Christ. The question to me became, "Can I believe God to perform His word of victory over my life just as I learned to trust Him to cleanse me from sin?"

Getting my test results back proved to me again that I could trust God to perform His word over my life. I made all A's. The question I thought I had bombed on my first exam was my greatest proof of God's faithfulness. I received a perfect 20 out of 20 points.

"As for God his way is perfect; the word of the Lord is flawless. He is a shield for all who take refuge in him. It is God who arms me with strength and makes my way perfect" (Psalm 18:30, 32).

It was important for me not only to pass my tests, but to pass this test of faith. My last semester would require that kind of foundation.

CHAPTER TWENTY-TWO

CHARTING MY LAST SEMESTER

"Let us run with perseverance the race marked out for us." (Hebrews 12:1)

Deciding on course selections each semester was an important task for me. It was like looking at a map and charting my course from one point to the next. There were certain roads I had to travel, but I was free to take some scenic routes, too. There was the fastest, most direct route. There was also a longer, but more interesting route.

Prayer and peace were my tour guides in making these selections. In observing many students, I discovered that they were only interested in the fastest route in getting through school. Their attitude was, "give me the interstates and I'll be happy." Sometimes they became so caught up in the time frame of their schooling, they couldn't fully absorb all that God had for them.

Personally, I wanted to find the balance between being a wise steward of my time, and yet, taking time to embrace all that the university had to offer. I wanted to run - but with patience - the course that God had marked out for me. If God had indeed marked out a course for me, it would be one that I could handle and yet one challenging enough to teach me to persevere. In my case, I decided to take an average of ten credit hours a semester throughout my graduate work, instead of the normal twelve. To compensate, I would worked steadily through the summers. This was my pace, of running with perseverance, and I liked it.

Every individual has his own pace. Learning to walk in that pace ensures maximum productivity and fulfillment for the student.

Working my last semester's courses into my individual pace was a challenge for me. Should I choose easy classes because it was my last semester? After all, I would be busy preparing for graduation and deserved a break. However, some of my favorite courses were offered my last full semester. They were also the hardest.

I did all my studies up until this point by faith in the greatness of my God. After much prayerful consideration, I opted for the more challenging path. Taking my thoughts to God once again I prayed, "Father, I have selected courses which will not only challenge me intellectually, but physically. But I am going to trust You to get me through - and with victory."

As I continued to take my thoughts and steps of faith to God, God continued to teach me His ways in my studies.

In the following months I experienced some of my greatest challenges and learned some of my greatest lessons. My course workload revealed to me even more of my weaknesses as well as the power of God. Most importantly, God taught me in a whole new way His ordering of my days.

Pacing has a lot to do with order. And God's order is a lot different than our own. Although I was a disciplined student, there were many times when I felt overwhelmed, disorganized, and burned-out.

If I was going to finish my three years at school with a peak experience, I was going to have to align myself with God's order in a way I had not yet known. In other words, I would have to enter into God's presence, guidance, and power at a deeper level. I was soon to find out what that ordering would entail, and the price I would have to pay to enter into it.

CHAPTER TWENTY-THREE

THE COMMAND OF WHOLEHEARTEDNESS

"In everything that he undertook in the service of God's temple and in obedience to the law and the commands, he sought his God and worked wholeheartedly. And so he prospered." (2 Chronicles 31:21)

There were many times when I came home from class feeling overwhelmed with my workload, or feeling the difficulty of an assignment. Instead of escaping or avoiding the task, I took my feelings to the Lord.

Of course, there were many ways my flesh wanted to vent its frustrations: television, ice-cream, sleep, sports, talking on the phone, to name a few. It was an ever increasing discipline in my communion with the Lord to take all of my emotions directly to him. He was worthy of having my whole heart, including my feelings towards my studies.

Coming home from school one day, I opened the door and immediately dove for the couch, collapsing into my favorite sack-out spot. "God, I feel overwhelmed with my studies! Help!"

I was too tired to move, so I just allowed myself some quality rest time. God spoke to my heart, "The problem isn't that you are overwhelmed with your studies. The problem is that you are underwhelmed with Me. Go worship Me."

God wanted to change my perspective of the situation and worship was the vehicle to do it. When I worship God, I enter into a dimension of faith where anything becomes possible. My focus is not on myself and my limitations, but on God who is all-powerful and all-knowing.

I began to develop a new discipline of worshipping God before I studied. I would turn on my stereo and blast Larnelle Harris' song, "How Excellent Is Thy Name O Lord." My brother had given me three-feet-high speakers for Christmas. I found out they worked very well! I played this song over and over again until I was ushered into the presence of God. It was not unusual for me to play this song ten or fifteen times, until it permeated my spirit.

Only when my picture of God became bigger than the picture of my studies and my own personal inadequacy would I sit down and begin to study. I would get the victory every time! True worship puts God in the big picture of things. True worship also clears your mind of all distracting thoughts because you are focused on God alone.

Many students sit down to study when they have everything on their mind but the task at hand: why their boyfriend or girlfriend didn't call them last night, what to fix for dinner, how they are going to pay the latest overdue bill. All these are valid concerns, but they can destroy your concentration. Instead of spending three hours trying to push away all those distracting thoughts, why not just worship God? Putting your focus on Him will still your spirit and clean out your brain at the same time. It will give you a "God's eye view" of the situation.

Worship became an essential element not only in my spiritual walk, but in my success as a student. It was my way of seeking God and giving Him my whole heart. It was also my way of stilling my spirit. Since stillness is essential to learning, worship became a powerful tool in my capacity to learn.

One of the ways you can integrate your faith and learning is to worship God for thirty minutes before you sit down to study. If you are new at this, find a worship tape that you like. It might be something classical like Handel's Messiah, or something contemporary like Hillsong worship tapes. Or it could be a favorite hymn or gospel music. Use whatever gets your mind off your work and onto God in a way that you enjoy. Put it on and begin to sing and worship along with the music.

Lift your heart and mind up to the Lord. Glide around the room and dance to it if you're looking for a good tension release. Allow Him to refresh your inner man with the power of his Spirit.

Give Him your whole heart - your mind, will, and emotions. Stay there until you feel a sense of peace, rest, and faith.

God is no respecter of persons. As He prospered King Hezekiah for seeking Him and working wholeheartedly, He will prosper you. He certainly began to prosper me in a whole new way in my studies!

CHAPTER TWENTY-FOUR

WAR, WORSHIP, AND SPRING WEATHER

"He has showed you, O man, what is good. And what does the Lord require of you? To act justly and to love mercy and to walk humbly with your God."
(Micah 6:8)

I struggled like everybody else when it came to studying for tests. At times I would much rather be outdoors, playing some sport in the spring sunshine, or dilly-dallying around with some friends, or just "chilling out" in front of the television. The hardest part of studying is the initial submission of my will to the discipline.

Preparing for Dr. Rea's exam during my last semester was no exception. It was a bright spring Saturday afternoon. All of nature was announcing its arrival and desire for all of humankind to enjoy its budding presence. My books were screaming for attention, too. "Oh no! The tug of war has begun! Do I choose buds or books? Help, God! Spring fever has hit me, and I need to prepare for this exam."

I glanced at my clock. It was twelve noon. "I could go out and play a while," reasoning with myself. For a few minutes I sat in my chair in silence. Deep within my heart I felt the Lord respond, "Veronica, you can choose one of two perspectives. You can see yourself with your head in your books all day long. Or you can see yourself spending all day with Me in the context of study. The choice is yours."

"Spending all day with You, God, is much more appealing to me than spending all day with my books. I like your perspective much better." The thought of God being with me all day long in the context of study was just enough perspective change for me to surrender to my task at hand - and start.

Eight and a half hours later I found myself so absorbed in my work that I hardly knew the day was passing me by. Although it took me many hours to "enter in," I found that blissful state of study where one looses all track of time. The distracting thoughts are gone. Every thought is absorbed into my mental computer. My mind is clear and soaking in volumes of information. This is intense!

Midnight rolled around. My mind was still in the groove, but my body was ready for sleep. I prayed, "'Lord, I have made a commitment not to study on Sunday. But I am so hungry for more of You in my studies that I would like to study tomorrow, too. In fact, is it okay not to go to church tomorrow? The anointing to study is so strong that I want to continue in this flow."

With the peace of God in my heart I ended my twelve hour study session. It flew by, after some struggle for the first several hours. I could hardly believe that just twelve hours prior to this time, study-ing was the last thing I wanted to do. Now it was all I wanted to do. My decision to surrender my will to God resulted in God's decision to enable me to study in the power of God.

My journal entry from Sunday, April 7, 1986, reads as follows: "My hand is shaking as I write. I woke up this morning feeling the anointing of God to study. I began to read in Micah and Hosea how God wanted intimate fellowship with His people. He wanted more than mere observance of requirements. In Micah 6:8, God talks about how He wanted deep communion, not ceremonial ex-actitude."

The problem with God's people in Hosea's day was a lack of the knowledge of God. This knowledge was just not simply knowing about God, but a failure to be properly related to Him in obedience and love. God's people did not need more information about God. They needed to fully respond to what they already knew. The Old Testament concept of knowledge meant living in close relationship with someone or something. Hence, fellowship was more important than strict obedience to the law.

In our studies to which we have been called, God is not so much concerned with our academic requirements: reading books, taking tests, writing papers. Although they are necessary, His ultimate interest is not in the outward doing of things. His ultimate desire is for us to bring to Him a devoted heart and to enter into an inner communion with Him.

We need to be willing to take the time to set ourselves apart to enter into this holy dimension. It can take me many hours to enter in, to become single-minded. When I am single-minded, I have no problem memorizing. It is only when I am double-minded that I have trouble concentrating, and my mind drifts. When I fix my eyes on Jesus, I become single-minded, in whatever I am doing.

How do you love someone unconditionally? One way is to give that person your full attention. A stranger is especially appreciative when you allow him to speak to you and tell you all about himself as you give him your full attention. How many times have you listened to someone and your thoughts are about three thousand miles away?

When we enter into study, we need to give God our full attention. We can love God with all our mind when we listen to Him talk to us about Himself through our studies. There is no greater or simpler act of devotion that we can we offer up to God as students than to turn our inner ear to Him. Whether the subject is Biblical Studies or Foreign Affairs, God is the Author of all Truth. If we seek to hear Him in the midst of the printed page, our time of drudgery will be turned into a time of worship acceptable to His glorious name.

My favorite definition of worship is found in *Dake's Commentary on the Bible*: "Worship is the direct acknowledgement of God, his nature, ways, attributes and claims, either by an outgoing expression of the heart in thanksgiving, or by deed done in such acknowledgement." I can worship God by praising Him, singing to Him, or expressing my thanks to Him.

Worshiping God also includes performing a deed that acknowledges who He is. The moment I offer up my study time to God as an acknowledgement of my love for Him, my study time becomes worship. The dividing line between the secular and the sacred is destroyed. Everything becomes material with which to lift up His great and glorious name! Praise God!

"My students are destroyed for lack of knowledge, (a lack of personal, intimate communion with God). He has showed you, O dear student, what is good. And what does the Lord require of you? To act justly and to love mercy and to walk humbly with your God as your Teacher."

As you begin to approach your studies as an act of worship to God, you will see your studies as something to offer up to God. As you submit your studies to God and invite Him to join you, you will grow in confidence and self-discipline. Your studies become a sacred pursuit. God is pleased and your academic requirements are fulfilled. It all begins with the heart!

CHAPTER TWENTY-FIVE

MERCY TRIUMPHS OVER COMPETITIVENESS

"I desire mercy, not sacrifice." (Matthew 12:7)

Academics is a competitive environment. Students vie for scholarships, G.P.A standing, favor with teachers, and availability of resources. We have all heard of stories of students hiding library books, cheating on exams, getting ahold of old exams, all to use for an unfair added advantage.

Is this the way a Christian student should operate? Hardly. Everything in the kingdom of God is upside down (or right side up, depending on your perspective) to the way the world operates. Using unfair, selfish, scheming means to excel is not God's way. Nor is engaging in an unhealthy competitiveness.

I must admit that I am a competitive person. I don't know if I am that way naturally. However, being in sports all my life has certainly drawn out that quality, sometimes to my benefit, and other times to my detriment. I also wanted to do well in school, but often found myself in a position where I was challenged to lay down my arms and serve my fellow student.

John was a dear friend of mine. We often sat on the library steps to ponder the wonders of the universe. I always liked talking to him because pondering partners are rare. You can talk to almost anybody about money, cars, sports, politics, fashion, or family. But how many people can you talk to about the "what if God" type questions?

John was also in one of my Biblical Studies classes. The day before a major exam, we left the classroom talking. I noticed John wasn't his usual energetic self. I asked him, "John, you look a little out of it. What's the matter?" John explained that he had been busy in ministry the last couple of days and did not have time to prepare for the exam. That was like saying a major snow storm was coming and all he had to wear was a bathing suit.

Tucked away within the dividers of my notebook was my systematized study sheet for the exam. I had devised my own effective system for learning material and preparing for exams. After each class I went home and immediately outlined the material from that day's class as well as the corresponding material from the book. Then I would memorize it the same day.

Using this system faithfully everyday, I would never have to worry about crash studying for an exam. Furthermore, when exam time came, I rarely had to review the book, or look at my class notes. Everything was already down on my own outline system. All I needed to do come exam time was to take out my daily notes and condense them.

For instance, if I had thirty pages worth of notes, I would condense those pages into ten pages, extracting key words and phrases. Then I would condense the ten pages into three pages, using the same process. My final step in exam preparation was to condense all of my notes into one page, using succinct words and acronyms. Using this system, I had learned the material not once, but multiple times. Going into the exam, I had a lot of confidence that I knew the material. Daily faithfulness to my note taking was the key.

So here I was facing John. I had totally prepared for this exam from the beginning of the course. My notes were meticulously in order and condensed for easy learning. Standing there sympathizing with my fellow student, the Holy Spirit whispered in my ear, "Veronica, are you going to share your notes with John?"

For a moment I was suspended in time. It was showdown time. The world's kingdom was in one corner of the boxing ring and God's kingdom was in the other. The bell was about to ring for the match to begin. Would I give the devil an opening round knockout blow, or would I stand complacently by and allow the world's system to chalk up another victory for self-centeredness?

The study demons were quick to give advice, "Veronica, you worked hard all semester for this exam. It's his own fault that he isn't prepared. Tell him you'll pray for him and go on your way. Helping him out will affect the grading curve to your detriment."

Another voice spoke quietly, "Without love I am nothing. Without love I gain nothing. Love is not self-seeking. It is more blessed to give than to receive. I desire mercy, not sacrifice." I finally made my choice.

"John, I just happen to have my notes with me. I understand your situation and would like to share my notes with you, if you would like them." John looked at me like he had just won the lottery, and said, "I would love to have your notes! Thanks so much!"

Mercy. God's way. I trusted in my heart that the God I served was big enough to bless me in my exam, regardless of how the rest of the class had prepared--or not prepared. Knowing that as I gave mercy it would come back to me, I gained a double victory. I not only did well on the test, but was thrilled to kick the study demons in the head, and grow in my desire to love God and others in my studies.

The way of competitiveness and jealousy says there's only a limited amount of glory to go around, and you have to fight to preserve your little bit.

The way of compassion and grace says that in God's economy, there's more than enough love and good stuff for everyone to prosper.

As a result of choosing God's way, I felt God's pleasure as a victory was won for his Kingdom. And I was about to reap a fresh dose of God's mercy in my next assignment.

LEARNING TO RECEIVE: PAPERS AND FINANCIAL GAIN ◊

CHAPTER TWENTY-SIX

LEARNING TO RECEIVE: PAPERS AND FINANCIAL GAIN

"Since the first day that you set your mind to gain understanding and to humble yourself before your God, your words were heard and I have come in response to them." (Daniel 10:12)

I wanted my next paper for Dr. Rea to be as significant as the first. After doing all my research, I sat down one Friday night to begin writing. Wanting my introduction to catch the reader's attention, I carefully selected every word.

Reviewing the first page, it all sounded very good but it didn't hook the reader. So I started writing introduction number two. After another hour I finished one more page of introduction. It was worse than the first! Both introductions sounded like they were written by a corpse! By now I was totally frustrated, and ready to pull out my hair.

Instead, I went to the Lord. "God, I don't understand. I have done my research, prayed, and even fasted over this paper. Why am I still struggling to write this research paper? Ugh! I thought I could depend on you, God. I've had it! I'm mad at You and I'm going to bed."

Dismissing any more thoughts about my paper, I shifted my focus to getting some sleep. With my mind clear and the mental wheels turned off for the day, I headed for bed.

All of a sudden a question popped into my mind. It was as if someone had entered my room and spoken to me. Arresting my attention, I knew it was the first line of my paper. In answering that question, the rest of my introduction flowed easily, line upon line. God had given me the inspiration and input I had asked of Him!

Curious as to why the evening had proceeded as it did, I asked the Lord, "Why couldn't the flow of my introduction come at the beginning of the evening? It would have made my paper writing a lot more enjoyable and easy. Besides, it would have saved me a lot of unnecessary time. Why did You wait until I was totally frustrated before You answered my prayer?"

The scripture, Daniel 10:12, came to mind. It was as if the Lord was saying to me, "Veronica, like Daniel, you have set your mind to gain understanding regarding the subject areas you are studying. Unlike Daniel, you have not humbled yourself to receive from Me. It was only until you were totally frustrated that you gave up relying on your own resources. At that point, you were in a position to receive from Me, so I could respond to you. Once you fill yourself with the research for writing a paper and pray, then learn to chill out and let Me work through you." Wow! Fill and chill. I liked that concept.

The next day I finished writing my introduction and began to tackle the rest of the paper. For some reason, I had trouble with the organization of the outline. Again I prayed, "Lord, now what do I do?" His response was, "Go worship Me." That wasn't the answer I was looking for. I pointed out the obvious, "God, I don't have time to worship You. This paper needs to be written!" God's reply was, "My ways are not obvious. They're higher than your ways. Now go worship."

I went into my living room and for the next forty-five minutes I worshiped God. I stayed there until my confusion left and I had peace in my heart regarding the direction in which to write my paper. This was the first time I had experienced the relationship between worship and organization of thoughts.

The entire paper was written in the context of worship. I wrote one section and then spent some time worshiping God. Worship produced peace. The subject I had peace about was the one I wrote about next. Although it took me a lot longer to complete the paper than normal, this was the way God directed me to write this particular paper. I soon found out what God had up his sleeve this time.

During the time of my writing I was experiencing some health problems which had been troubling me for about a year. Hesitant to see a doctor because I had no health insurance, I finally consented. After a series of tests the only thing I left the hospital with was a doctor bill for approximately $1,000. They could find nothing wrong with me. "Okay, God, you know my need. I trust You to pay for this."

The same day I received an unexpected check in the mail from my mother for $400. On my way to chapel I asked one of my girlfriends to pray for God's provision. "How much money do you need?" she asked. After telling her, she responded, "I have been saving some money for some needy people, but I would not give it to them until they asked. You were one of the people God placed on my heart a while ago to help." She pulled out her checkbook and handed me a check. My bill was almost paid off!

On top of my hospital bill, I also had my local doctor bill. During my office visit my doctor asked me about areas of stress in my life. I mentioned school. Somehow we struck up a conversation about the paper I was writing.

For the next thirty minutes I explained to him the concepts in my paper, which I did not think were anything profound. Apparently he thought they were, because he sat at the edge of his seat spellbound, soaking up every word. When I finished speaking, he stood up and approached me. Thinking that he was going to shake my hand, I was surprised when he reached into his pocket and pulled out his wallet.

"You have come here to pay me for my time for ministering to you. Now I am going to pay you for your time for ministering to me. What you have spoken to me today was the answer to a prayer I have been praying for a long time. Today my life has been changed." My doctor then pulled out some money and handed me the cash to pay my bill.

Did you catch that? My own doctor gave me the money to pay for my doctor bill! I never knew a paper would merit financial gain!

I laughed all the way home. "God, you are so funny! I never know what to anticipate with You. You take things that are boring, dry, and a struggle, and do something with them far beyond my imagination. When I give you my chaos, You speak my world and all my papers into existence for Your glory! I'm so glad I made You my Study Buddy. You're the best!"

God wanted to do something significant in someone's life that I knew nothing about. It was through my obedience to worship Him in the midst of writing my paper that prepared the way for my doctor to be touched in a profound way. God knew that my doctor needed an answer to prayer and that I needed a financial blessing. God proved Himself to the two of us in yet another eternal and unforgettable way.

God is more than able to take the mundane and infuse it with His majesty. He took my illness, my need for financial help, my paper writing, my anger and frustration, and my desire to bless Him and others. Then He mixed it all up with His omnipotence and mercy, sparked my academic life, answered the prayer of another saint, and eventually healed my body completely.

Humbling myself wasn't such a bad idea, after all. Thank you, Jesus, for teaching me to fill and chill--and then thrill--at seeing You answer prayer.

CHAPTER TWENTY-SEVEN

ACADEMICS AND PRACTICING THE PRESENCE OF GOD

"Have I not commanded you? Be strong and courageous. Do not be terrified; do not be discouraged, for the Lord your God will be with you wherever you go." (Joshua 1:9)

One of the greatest times of learning for me was studying for tests. My aim was not only to know the information for the exam, but to learn it for my own personal and future benefit. Above all, my times of exam preparation were special devotional times.

I remember praying for my first exam in my last class with Dr. Williams, my theology professor. "Lord, I pray that You will use my efforts and heart to bless Dr. Williams in this test. In fact, I pray You bless his socks off through this test. God, I also want to know You better through this experience. It would also be nice to get an A."

Seeking the Lord and working wholeheartedly was my way of going about all of my school work. This gave me peace and confidence before God when I entered into each exam.

There were times, however, that I would catch myself becoming very anxious over a test. It was during those times that I would stop and say, "Lord, I know You are with me during this exam just as much as You were with me during the preparation time. Right now

I thank You for Your peace. I refuse to take tests in anxiety anymore, because it is not a part of my inheritance in You."

What a new experience for me to take tests in peace! The peace came in knowing that God's presence was with me--and in knowing that His love for me was unconditional.

No matter how well or how poorly I did, His love for me remained the same. And even if I blew it--even if I failed--the universe would not fall apart. God was holding it together, and He would always be there to hold me together too, no matter what. With that in mind, I could relax. It was this kind of experience that led me to know God better - and to love Him more.

I also practiced the presence of God when I typed papers. Let's face it, typing is boring. Nowadays, one can create and type papers at the same time, thanks to computer technology. When I went to graduate school, I was still handwriting my papers, then typing them. How I hated to sit down and spend needless time on the typewriter!

One night I was very anxious typing a paper. I wanted to go home and relax. The last place I wanted to be on a Friday night was in the library finishing up a paper. Then I caught myself. "Veronica, God is with you just as much in the typing of this paper as He is during a relaxing Friday night chilling out. Why don't you stop and create a Spirit-filled environment for yourself?"

I paused and prayed. "Jesus, thank you that You are with me right now. Forgive me for not inviting Your presence into this time. Be with me." Then I turned on some worship music in my little study room and thoroughly enjoyed the rest of my time on the typewriter.

Henry Drummond in his book, *The Greatest Thing in the World*, said it best: "Religion is the inspiration of the secular life." True religion is not so much that we ascend to God, but that He comes down to meet us where we are, to bring the majestic into the mundane. As I practiced the presence of God in the details of my study life, I discovered a richer, more meaningful experience than I ever dreamed possible.

People try to find fulfillment in knowledge and it does not exist there. King Solomon was the wisest man who ever lived, but he expresses the futility of knowledge for its own sake in the book of Ecclesiastes:

> "Then I applied myself to the understanding of wisdom, and also of madness and folly, but I learned that this, too, is a chasing after the wind. For with much wisdom comes much sorrow; the more knowledge, the more grief."
> (Ecclesiastes 1:17, 18)

He concludes with the observation, "Of making many books there is no end, and much study wearies the body" (Ecclesiastes 12:12). Only in Jesus Christ can we find true life and fulfillment. In other words, there is no life in academics. There is only true life in Jesus Christ.

I prepared for my second and third exams with Dr. Williams in the same way I did for the first, and then I prayed the same prayer. "Lord, I want to know You in the midst of my test preparation. I want to do well, and I want You to bless Dr. Williams' socks off again. Holy Spirit, I know that will happen if I can get another 100 per cent on his exam! It's not important to me to make a 100 per cent, but I know that would bless my teacher."

God answered my prayer with overwhelming success. Not only did I make a 100 on my first exam, but I made perfect scores on all my exams. Dr. Williams said that had never happened in the history of that course. Truly he was blessed, and I was blessed. I loved God all the more in knowing that He had heard my prayer and honored it.

CHAPTER TWENTY-EIGHT

THE BEST WAY TO KILL A DRAGON

"There is no fear in love. But perfect love drives out fear, because fear has to do with punishment." (1 John 4:18)

In early May of my last semester, the School of Biblical Studies held a commissioning service. It was a special time of fun and sending forth for the graduates. I was in the class.

The dean of the school addressed us with an inspiring message about the Apostle Paul. He emphasized how Paul was eager to preach the Gospel and wasn't ashamed because he was a debtor. Paul had been given something--the message of salvation--to give to others. He would be held accountable for what he did with that great gift. It was Paul's recognition of what he had been given and what he owed God in return that made him a debtor. That recognition gave him the boldness, passion, and drive to share the Gospel. Nothing stopped Paul in his mission, not even the threat of death.

Where does such fearlessness come from? It begins with the love of God shed abroad in our hearts. Overwhelmed with the thought of that love, and the realization of our own unworthiness to receive it apart from Christ, we are moved to share it with others. An invisible but unconquerable force compels us to reach beyond our own limitations and self-protectiveness to others.

Every child of God has the love of God in him. The courage to act out of God's unconditional acceptance - and not out of fear - gives one the power to reach beyond himself and achieve far more than he dreamed possible. The essence of this truth would be God's word to me at the commissioning service.

A professor and his wife laid hands on me. She was impressed to speak the following words to me: "Veronica, fear is the only thing that will ever hold you back. Keep pushing fear back and nothing will be impossible to you. *Nothing will be impossible for you!* Remember, perfect love casts out all fear."

Another professor finished by praying that the path would be cleared for God's will to transpire in my life. He also prayed that God's will would be the joy, delight, and desire of my heart. If only they could have shared my walk with God in my studies to know just how right on their prayers were, not only for my future, but even for my present experience.

The one life principle I have determined to incorporate into every area of my life is this: The best way to kill a dragon is to walk right up and stab it in the throat. Fear is the dragon that keeps dreams, gifts, and talents locked up. My policy always has been to do the thing I feared if I thought I was being held back from an experience I really wanted.

If I feared speaking, I got behind a microphone and made myself talk. If I feared singing, I joined the choir. If I feared raising my hand in class to share my opinion, I would force myself to do it. I absolutely refuse to be dominated by the fear dragon.

As a child of God, I knew that "God did not give us a spirit of timidity, but a spirit of power, of love and of self-discipline" (2 Timothy 1:7). To be a Christian student, I had to learn how to be motivated by Christian motives in my work, and fear was not one of them.

Consider what fear is:

F: false

E: evidence

A: that appears

R: real.

Fear is a smoke screen. It says, "You can't do that. You don't have what it takes." My way out of fear and inadequacy was to say, "That's right, in myself I can't. But in God I can do all things and I *do* have what it takes." Then I could face up to my particular fear, one step at a time, and stab that dragon right in the throat. The sweet taste of the thrill of victory over the kingdom of darkness in my life was always worth the risk of facing my every fear.

I remember one particular instance of overcoming fear that taught me a lot about slaying dragons. For many months the Lord had stirred me to start a single women's ministry at the university. It would be a delight to my heart to see women get together, minister to one another, and use their gifts and talents in service.

It was no problem for me to gather together some of my friends to write a constitution, advertise for the first event, and prepare the program. However, getting in front of a group of women and speaking made me want to go home, crawl into a closet and hide. Not me, God. Like Moses who was afraid to speak, I wanted God to send an Aaron instead. The closer the time came, the more terrified I became.

Since my closet was a bit too stuffed with clothes to crawl into, I decided to retreat to the little chapel before the first meeting. "Jesus, You know I'm not doing this because I feel adequate. Lord, I submit my fears and insecurities to You. Be with me as I lead these women in the meeting. Okay, Holy Spirit, let's go!"

Fighting back the tears, I headed for the auditorium. After greeting the women, I opened with prayer. Speechless, all I could pray was the same prayer I prayed in the chapel, "Lord, you know I'm not standing here because I feel adequate." Then I burst into tears in front of all those women! Groping for what to do next, I looked up, peered around the room and asked, "Does anybody have a Kleenex?"

What followed my initial tear-jerking introduction was a great meeting. Afterwards, one of the women commented to me that she was hesitant to come to another single women's gathering if all we were interested in was staring at our navels. When I was vulnerable enough to cry and admit my inadequacy before everyone, her heart was touched. She knew that we were genuine and she sincerely wanted to be a part of the group. What made me feel stupid (crying before the group) gave one young woman a sense of belonging. God works in strange and wonderful ways.

Having the experience of speaking every month in a safe environment gradually built up my confidence. Each opportunity I had to speak was another step in stabbing my dragon of fear in its throat. Before long, the dragon died. I can now speak to thousands without any plaguing fear.

I used the same process in overcoming my fear of raising my hand in class. First, I would recognize that my behavior was based on fear. Knowing that fear was not a part of who I was in God, I would submit it to the Lord as my next step. Finally, I would step out in faith, one step at a time, following His leading.

In the case of raising my hand in class, I would say to myself, "Veronica, you have something worth saying. Now raise your hand and say it." Sometimes my left arm would have to push up the right arm, but I would make myself do it. Then I would pat myself on the back for another victory! Each little victory would give me the platform to go on to bigger victories.

My presentation of my graduate portfolio to the university community would be one of my greatest challenges in overcoming my fear of speaking. How would I kill the fear dragon this time?

CHAPTER TWENTY-NINE

FREEDOM TO FAIL

*"For you did not receive a spirit that makes you a slave again to fear, but
you received the Spirit of sonship. And by him we cry 'Abba, Father.'"*
(Romans 8:15)

The day finally came to share my portfolio with the university
community. For my graduate portfolio I decided to develop an
eight-week course on the renewed mind in academics. The course
was a combination of biblical truths, the testimony of my walk with
Christ in my studies, and an application for students to follow
Christ for themselves.

Although I was overcoming my fear of speaking before groups
in general, this was a different case. I would be sharing publicly
what I had been developing and utilizing in a rather private fashion.
I felt like I would be exposing the inner workings of my heart and I
certainly wanted it to be received.

Anxious to express my inner thoughts to God, I headed over to
a friend's house. In the back of her house was a lake. One of my
favorite places to hear from God was out on the middle of her lake.

Climbing into her paddle boat, I felt like one of the disciples
getting into the boat to meet with Jesus on the water! Once out in
the middle of the lake, I grabbed my Bible and prayed, "Jesus,
tomorrow I am sharing the heartbeat of all my labor while at this

university. I'm scared and feeling rather inadequate. Please speak to me. You know I want to do excellently, and I want my presentation to be received."

Pausing for a few moments to hear from God, I was surprised at His response. I felt like He said, "Veronica, if you fall flat on your face tomorrow, I would still be pleased with you."

Wow! God wanted me to know, once again, His unconditional love in everything I did. Receiving those words set me free to fail. Ultimately, however, they set me free to succeed. In my heart I knew that I was a child of God. No matter how I performed in my audience's eye, God wanted me to know ahead of time that I was surrounded by His embrace.

The acknowledgement of God's love for me also set me free to love my audience. Instead of fearing their criticism, which is really fearing their judgment, I decided to adopt the opposite perspective. My aim would be to minister to them. The focus would not be on how they would look at me, but on how I would look at them. The only thing that truly mattered was my desire to love my audience and to minister to them. My motivation to love my listeners set me free from performance-orientation and fear in my speaking.

I felt my portfolio presentation was one of the best and easiest presentations I ever gave. My decision to be God-conscious instead of man-conscious made all the difference. Coming to this level in my speaking was not instantaneous. It took about two years of diligent and progressive effort. God led me step by step in conquering my fears and inadequacies. Sometimes students give up too easily, or compare themselves to others and short circuit their own growth. Start where you are and build from there.

My last paper was also my best in terms of the ease with which I wrote the paper. Recalling how I had struggled--sometimes intensely--with articulating my thoughts, I continued to work on expressing my heart in simple academic style. This particular paper seemed to flow right off the press of my heart and mind and onto the written page. It was another victory in conquering the academic kingdom of my heart.

Outward academic success in the form of grades and mastering the subject matter is important. Inward victory in our hearts is even more important because that fruit is eternal. It shapes our character and our future with God. What we are in private is what we are in public. Freedom to fail, freedom to succeed, confidence in God, freedom to accept our strengths and weaknesses is precisely the stuff that God uses to shake the kingdom of darkness. Consider an experience of mine on a Florida golf course.

One of my friends from Orlando invited me to play golf at Arnold Palmer's course, Bay Hill. The course is magnificent, but the most outstanding feature I will always remember is the alligators. They think they own the course! You could be walking down the fairway on a water hole and right in the middle of the fairway is this raving reptile roaming freely over my territory. To one of my playing partners, my presence would prove to be like that feisty alligator in the fairway.

My playing partners were all stockbrokers, and it was interesting for me to observe the way they handled the stress of their high-pressured occupation. It was even more interesting for them to observe this golfer set free to play.

If I hit a good shot I would express some kind of joy or glee like, "Wow, that was a great shot!" I didn't say this because I was arrogant, but rather because I had finally learned to like my swing as imperfect as it was. Hitting a good shot when I didn't expect to was an especially joyful experience to me. On one par four, I hit my third shot over the green. I hit my next shot in the sand trap. My trap shot went flying over the green again. With the same kind of joyful glee I exuded over a good shot, I exclaimed, "What a terrible shot!"

One of the stockbrokers turned to me with the most puzzling look, and said, "You have the best attitude." His response to my attitude was like seeing an alligator in the middle of the fairway. You knew it was there, but it didn't seem like it belonged there. My joyful attitude coming through a bad shot was something else that didn't seem to fit. It shook him up.

Unaware of how I was affecting him, I replied, "Jesus set me free, and He can set you free, too. By the way, why do you smoke cigarettes?" He confessed that smoking was a release from the pressure of his job. I told him, "Jesus can set you free and be your release so you don't need those cigarettes." I encouraged him further in the Lord.

The point is, what caught the attention of my fellow golfer was not the technical perfection of my swing, but the inner man set free to praise God regardless of the execution of the shot. I wasn't even conscious of what was happening, until he noticed my freedom in Christ. It was this freedom, not a perfect swing, that bore witness to this golfer and gave me the opportunity to minister to him.

Whether on the course or in the classroom, God wants us to walk as His sons and daughters, free from fear and free to express His love in everything we do. Before I graduated, I would find out just how important loving God with all my mind would be to Him.

CHAPTER THIRTY

GRADUATION HURTS

"Set your minds on things above, not on earthly things." (Colossians 3:2)

Have you ever expected to be rewarded for something and then watched that award get handed to someone else?

Shortly before graduation I came across a memo which listed the student commencement speakers. More than anything, I wanted to be one of them. My name was not on the list. Nor was I selected to be the outstanding student in communication. I was crushed.

God had honored my desire and goal of making a perfect 4.0 G.P.A through two master's programs. It was in my heart to serve my university. I endeavored to love God and others in everything I did. But I did not receive the award I expected. The School of Biblical Studies honored me with their outstanding student award. Because I felt my contribution to the School of Communication was no less, I naturally assumed I would receive their outstanding student award as well. In fact, I had counted so heavily on receiving this double honor that when it was given to another student, I was devastated.

Heartbroken, I cried. "God, I know You love me and You are sovereign. I don't understand this major disappointment. I never thought I would feel such hurt at graduation time. Why did this happen?"

Be careful when you make a commitment to God to do something solely for His glory. He will be sure to test your heart.

Without question, God was testing my heart. "Veronica, did you really do all of this for My glory, or is your devotion tainted by desire for man's glory and recognition?" His question pierced my heart.

Whatever the answer to His question was, God wanted to honor my prayer. But He didn't do it the way I expected. Instead, He made certain that I would not be caught up in pride and man's glory by giving me another experience of brokenness.

God comforted my heart and reassured me of His grace through another student who told me the following story. There was once a missionary on a ship coming home from a long journey. He had spent many long years serving the Lord and enduring through many trials and hardships. There were also a lot of distinguished dignitaries on board. When the ship arrived at the port, all the distinguished guests were applauded and honored for being home. The missionary was discouraged and perplexed as to why he did not receive any honors or awards for his service. When he put his question before his mother, she replied, "Son, it's because you haven't come home yet."

God had not forgotten me. He was saving the best for last. But He did have some important honors in store for me.

CHAPTER THIRTY-ONE

GOD'S FINAL EXAM

"Again Jesus said, 'Simon son of John, do you truly love me?'" (John 21:16)

Our final exam in our Book of Hebrews class was canceled. I was delighted because it gave me more time to finish my paper. Once I handed the paper in, the professor was quick to grade it and return it. Reviewing the paper, I noticed a lot of lines, marks, and comments on it. All of his remarks and corrections were valid and helpful. But all my mistakes made me feel terribly inadequate.

Once home I decided to have my devotional time since I had forgotten to get to it in the morning. The heading for the devotional I was reading for that specific day was "Final Exam." How appropriate! Although the professor had canceled His final, God was giving me one of His own.

The thrust of the teaching for that day was on loving and obeying God. The scripture from 1 Corinthians 16:22 was a piercing one, "If anyone does not love the Lord--a curse be on him. Come, O Lord!" Not your usual "bless me" word.

The devotional also mentioned the account of Noah in Genesis 6:9-22. Noah was instructed by God to build an ark. God gave Noah very specific instructions on how to do it. It took Noah many years to finish the assignment, but he faithfully completed his task. Noah's obedience to God was credited to him as righteousness, for Noah did according to all that God had commanded. Obedience was the test of Noah's love for God.

Every person's final exam question will be based on the same principle of obedience and question: "Do you love the Lord Jesus Christ?" A quote from Charles Hodge drove home the point for me:

"If we love Christ, we shall be zealous for his glory. Any neglect or irreverence shown our Savior will wound our hearts. Any honor rendered him will give us delight. The son who loves his father desires to please him, to do his will, obey his command, observe his counsel, always and in all places. So those who love Christ keep his commandments. This is the test of love for Christ."

What God was trying to impart to me was that His final exam was not based on my academic honors, or lack of them, my IQ, or my impressive G.P.A. His final exam question to me was, "Veronica, do you love Me?" It was the same final exam question Jesus asked Peter after everything they had been through together.

In response, I expanded God's final exam with asking myself a few more questions. Did I love God during my several years as a graduate student? Did I take all the classes He wanted me to take? Did I follow Him? Did I wholly dedicate myself to Him? Did I seek Him with all my heart in my school work? Did I obey Him when He was trying to teach me something? Did I love Him by loving myself? Did I love Him by loving others?

In the depth of my heart, I could answer yes to all those questions. Tears welled up from within confirming to me that I had passed God's final exam! What a staggering thought.

More than receiving any academic award, I wanted the award of God's approval. The price of God's high calling. The blessing of hearing Jesus' words was the most cherished award I could receive. Those words I heard loud and clear, "Well done, my good and faithful servant." My tears of discouragement from the results of my paper were once again turned into a different kind of tears--tears of gratitude and joy. I had come to know the love of God. And that was the best graduation present anyone could ever give me.

CHAPTER THIRTY-TWO

ONE GOOD TURN DESERVES ANOTHER

"O Lord, our Lord, how excellent is your name in all the earth!" (Psalm 8:1, KJV)

Commencement time came and so did my chance to walk across the platform and receive my two diplomas. One was for a master's degree in Communication, the other for a master's in Biblical Studies. I was the only student in the entire school to graduate with three stars next to her name. The stars were for a perfect 4.0 G.P.A through two graduate degrees.

I honestly thought the biggest thrill of my journey through academics would be the accomplishment of my goal. For three years I had diligently pursued my desire. The day had finally arrived to celebrate its attainment. But the joy of my achievement lasted only a split second as I walked across the platform to accept my diplomas. Like a quick gust of wind, my culminating moment blew in and out. What a letdown.

What will remain with me forever, however, is the joy of discovering God in my academic walk. That experience I will take with me through all eternity. My education was a great one, no doubt, but the relationship with my Teacher was even greater. Earthly achievements will pass away, but coming to a deeper knowledge of my heavenly Father will never fade away.

As I already mentioned, my father died when I was fifteen. I loved him, but I never knew what made him tick. There were few father-daughter moments to look back on and treasure. Regretfully, I did not truly know him.

Ever since he died I've always thought what an absolute tragedy it would be to go throughout my entire lifetime here on earth and never truly know my heavenly Father.

Many sincere Christians make the mistake of thinking that salvation is simply a ticket to get into heaven. What they fail to realize is that salvation is a restoration of relationship with the Living God. The promise of God to tabernacle with His people is a major theme from Genesis through Revelation. God's desire is to dwell in the midst of us!

Learning to walk with God in my studies was my most cherished treasure. I can forever look back in my chats with God and say, "Lord, do you remember when You first wanted to be with me in my acting class? How about the time You healed that person through reading my paper? That was pretty amazing. You even showed me Your humor with my doctor. Do you remember that day, God? How about the first time I let go and trusted the Holy Spirit in my test-taking? That was such a big step for me. To You, it was probably like seeing Your daughter walk for the first time. Or how about all Your miraculous provisions of money? Just when I thought I hit a dead end, You pulled out another of your cattle on a thousand hills, traded it in, and found some creative way to get the cash to me. You're something else, Father."

One of the most special and surprising moments with God happened during our graduation quad party. All the students who lived in our section of grad housing celebrated with a party out in the courtyard area. It was your typical hamburger hoopla, until my next door neighbor announced he had a song to sing.

Everyone gathered around. Bill cranked up his stereo, and announced, "This song is for Veronica. It's a graduation present." A song for me! This was getting good.

Then Bill began to sing Larnelle Harris' song, "How excellent is Your name O God, how excellent is Your name. The heavens and earth together proclaim how excellent is Your name...."

I was stunned. This was *my* song--the soundtrack of my time spent worshiping God in my studies, the track I had used to rediscover my reason for being here. How did he know?

When Bill finished singing, he explained, "Veronica, when you were playing this song over and over again in your living room, I was on the other side of the wall wondering what on earth you were doing. You played it so many times, that whenever you would sing it, I would join in and sing, too. So I decided to buy the tape, and sing it back to you for a graduation present."

Joy surged through my heart! Up until graduation I sang that song to God. Now God was singing the song back to me through Bill as an expression of His gratitude and pleasure. One good turn deserves another. Jesus, You are so wonderful!

The excellency of *His* name. Have you ever thought about it? The world is bent on pursuing excellence for the sake of excellence, so that man can build a reputation. If Christians aren't careful, they will adopt the same mindset. The true heart of Christianity is to uphold the excellency of His name, not our own. It is to honor the name of God, at whatever cost.

What I was coming to know in my studies was the majesty of knowing my God as my Teacher, Guide, Comforter, Encourager, Friend, Insurance Agent, Banker, Mover of Professors' hearts, Reminder, and Lover of my soul. Instead of simply loving God, I fell in love with God in this process. Growing in intimacy with God, I came to know His love, mercy, truth, humor, and commands.

I also paid a heavy price for it. Instead of developing a lot of friendships and social life, I poured myself into my spiritual life. Did the other areas suffer? Honestly, yes. There were many lonely days. But the high call of loneliness is sometimes the only road on which God can reveal Himself to us. It's a path where nobody else can travel because He wants the relationship to be exclusive. He wants each of us to know Him as He is.

It is my prayer that you will allow the love of God already shed abroad in your heart by the Holy Spirit to express itself in a new way in your studies and in your everyday life. The only thing awaiting you is your decision to have your very own divine adventure with the Creator of the Universe. He is ready to speak your academic world into existence. All He wants is a little chaos, confusion, and the soil of a humble heart where He can work His miracles in and through your life.

Now it's your turn to step out of performance-orientation and into His marvelous presence in your learning journey. Here's the baton! Now run your race to win!

Would you like to learn more about Spirit-led Study?

Special Bonus – **Free Academic Success Videos**

Receive 10 free faith-based academic success videos.

Join the God's Way to an A Facebook group to get instant access to Veronica's video trainings!

Facebook/God's Way to an A

Veronica' signature on-line course, God's Way to an A

God's Way to an A is Veronica's signature discipleship course on learning how to become a Spirit-led student. This 7 lesson curriculum includes a 170 page study manual, 7 videos, 7 audios, and live recorded coach trainings. Students have soared to the head of the class with this self-study curriculum.

Godswaytoana.com/class

Blog: **veronicakaraman.com**

Invite Veronica to speak at your school, church, or organization for your spiritual emphasis week, new student orientation, one day workshops, and teacher trainings.

Contact: veronica@truechampioncoaching.com

www.ingramcontent.com/pod-product-compliance
Lightning Source LLC
LaVergne TN
LVHW051245080426
835513LV00016B/1756